# ACCOUNTING FOR LIFE

## *A Journey Heavenward*

***I press on toward the goal to win the prize for which God has called me heavenward in Christ Jesus.***
***Philippians 3:14***

**TERESITA "*Tess*" PAJE, MBA**

Published by
Innovo Publishing, LLC
www.innovopublishing.com
1-888-546-2111

Providing Full-Service Publishing Services for
Christian Organizations & Authors: Hardbacks, Paperbacks,
eBooks, Audio Books, & iPhone Application Books



ISBN 13: 978-1-936076-12-3
ISBN 10: 1-936076-12-8

Cover Design & Interior Layout: Innovo Publishing, LLC

Printed in the United States of America
U.S. Printing History

First Edition: November 2009

# ACKNOWLEDGMENTS

This book was written to share with each reader my heart's desire for people to come to know God and be rightly related to Him. With the realization of this book, I therefore solemnly acknowledge my Father in heaven for His grace, guidance, protection, and unconditional love. In His name, I pray for wisdom, blessing, and revelation to every word transcribed here. Each day that I spent writing this book, I felt God's presence, through the Holy Spirit, helping me to know what to write. My personal encounter with God through the writing of this book was very reassuring and alive, thus every Scripture was God's breath and inspiration to me. Indeed, God's Word was magnified, enabling me to access our Savior Jesus Christ. God's epiphany was attested by the life transformations of my husband and me. To my loving Father in heaven I dedicate this book.

With appreciation I thank my husband, Rey, for giving me his blessing to share his very personal life testimony. It almost dragged me to the end of my rope, but my Father in heaven rescued me. I now look at this particular experience as an affirmation of God's relationship with me. Indeed, I am thankful to my Father in heaven for allowing me to reach the breaking point for my own good.

For the love and understanding of my husband and my daughters, Trisha and Karina, I love you. Thank you to my family, friends, and clients for their prayers, moral support, and time spent listening to all the excitement I had while writing this book. I will ever be grateful and thankful to the following friends, who are near and dear to my heart and who, in one way or the other, either directly or indirectly, contributed their time and effort to this book: Dr. Bettye Albritton, Mrs. Fedelie Punsalan-Lutz, Dr. Myrna Lazaga, Mrs. Delia Jamir, Dr. Akunna Winston, Ms. Lucia Tuquero, Mrs. Vicki Bentley (my pastor's wife), Mrs. Beth Sanders, Mrs. Margie Alberto, Mrs. Fely Cueva, and, most especially, Mrs. Aida Laxa with her very touching personal testimony on the subject of hope.

Again, thank you to my Father in heaven!

# CONTENTS

# INTRODUCTION

## *Author's Perspective*

What's happening to our American dream of owning a house, funding our retirements, and saving for our kids' college funds? With all these financial worries—housing crisis, rising cost of living, economic downturn, loss of jobs—should we now give up those dreams? I must say, "Certainly not." Then what should we do?

First of all, it is my intent to share my personal perspectives, which I trust will give hope and encouragement. What's happening in our economy is a worldwide problem that has contributed to a lot of frustration, anger, worry, and fear. I strongly believe that the economic crisis most likely was brought by the violation of God's principles of handling money and possessions. My thinking is that this entire crisis was driven by people's personal greed.

In retrospect, this could be the most opportune moment to know who our Creator is and to take this opportunity to recommit ourselves to Him. This book, *Accounting For Life—A Journey Heavenward,* will guide and direct us to a lifestyle far beyond what money can buy and to a journey of pursuing intimacy with God. If we can focus on what Ecclesiastes 2:11 says—"Yet when I surveyed all that my hands had done and what I had toiled to achieve, everything was meaningless, a chasing after the wind, nothing was gained under the sun"—then we can begin to understand God's plan for our lives.

As a financial advisor, I tell people to plan for their future with regard to their finances. But we also must be reminded by Proverbs 16:3, "Commit to the Lord whatever you do and your plans will succeed." Our lifestyle has changed drastically in the last few years--partially because of the many economic opportunities that have been available to us, along with the demand of consumerism. In the end, it was far too overwhelming. But one thing I can assure you is that God's plan for us far outweighs all these things.

Always make plans, and don't let your dreams be washed away. Only this time, remember where to go to find timeless wisdom about handling your finances. Proverbs 16:9 says, "In his heart a man plans his course, but the Lord determines his steps." Plunging home values, a declining stock market, failing banks, and falling value of the dollar seem to be our biggest worries. But aren't we forgetting Someone of intrinsic value, the very One who created us?

What could be more important and practical than learning the fundamentals of life based on God's Word? With these practical fundamentals of life, we learn to follow truthful and timeless Scriptures that will guide us toward the right path of life. In Proverbs 3:5-6, we are reminded, "Trust in the Lord with all your heart and lean not on your own understanding; in all your ways acknowledge him and he will make your path straight."

Our life on earth is a journey. For some people it's a short journey, and for others it could be a long journey. Only God determines when we are born and when we will die. During our life journey on earth, we are accountable to God for how we live our lives. This is what I present in *Accounting for Life—A Journey Heavenward.* Every day of our lives on earth, we account for our actions, words, thoughts, and deeds as we interact with others in this world. Accounting to God for our very lives seems overwhelming, but it also could be very rewarding. It does, however, reflect how we manifest our lives to God.

When I was attending business college, I majored in accounting. Having studied accounting, I was always fascinated by how we made sure that all business book entries balanced and that every financial transaction was accounted for. Even in my previous job as an auditor, I had to consistently provide accountability for all the financial records of business transactions and to report all operating results correctly and accurately to the owners and stockholders of the company. In our lives, then, should we not also give account for our daily personal activities to our Creator who owns us? According to Romans 14:12, "So then, each of us will give an account of himself to God."

Let me share with you the meaning of accounting from the business perspective, as defined by the *American Heritage Dictionary of the English Language* (4th edition, Houghton Mifflin Company): "Accounting is the bookkeeping methods involved in making financial records of business transactions and in the preparation of statements concerning the assets, liabilities and operating results of a business."

On the other hand, accounting for life is the act of keeping accounts of all our daily decisions and activities relating to our actions, thoughts, words, and deeds in such a manner that these activities glorify God. Accounting to God is accounting for our actions, words, thoughts, and deeds in all facets of our lives (spiritual, physical, emotional, and financial), thus maintaining a godly relationship with the Lord, as we journey heavenward.

In Luke 12:48, Jesus said, "From everyone who has been given much, much will be demanded and from the one who has been entrusted with much, much will be asked." Therefore, we are all expected to keep account of all our life entries, based on our level of serving others. My pastor once said in one of his Sunday messages that he is more accountable to God than anybody in the congregation because he is the leader of the church. I certainly agree with him. But since I also teach a Bible study, much will be required of me as well. I make sure that what I determine to accomplish in the Bible study will all be centered on God and His glory.

Without maintaining proper accounting for life, it is possible neither to ascertain blessings nor to get to know our Maker and His purpose for us. Accounting for life is a discipline that touches our daily lives. Knowing that our lives are completely in God's hands, we must be accountable to Him at all times. Therefore, when things go wrong, we need to turn to God. We then pray, ask for forgiveness, and put our trust in Him.

***Heavenly Father:***

*Please help us not to let our dreams be washed away*
*Just because of the uncertainty of the economy,*
*But to make this moment be the opportunity*
*To build personal relationship with You, dear Almighty.*

*Please remind us to be accountable to your kingdom,*
*Relating our actions, words, thoughts, and deeds*
*To ascertain blessings and to know Your purpose*
*As we journey toward pursuing intimacy with You,*
*Almighty God. AMEN.*

## *The Book's Purpose and Life Application*

This book provides practical fundamentals of life based on the Bible. These Biblical fundamentals will help us to understand more deeply our relationship with God and to develop intimacy with Him. God's commands in the Scriptures direct us to His way, His purpose, and His result. He therefore holds us accountable for our daily decision making as reflected through our actions, words, thoughts, and deeds.

Through the Holy Spirit, we strive to find God's purpose in our lives. Allowing God to take control of our lives will lead us to that purpose. If we are to live a life His way, doing His work and seeking His results, then ultimately we are giving honor, praise, and glory to God our Creator. Life application of these Biblical principles enables us to manage our lives in accordance with God's plan for our lives and for the lives of others, thus ultimately glorifying God. Life, in itself, is a form of giving and taking that revolves around our daily activities. How do we account for these? What are our sources and resources? How much can we give versus how much we can receive? And what are our priorities?

Having studied accounting, along with my experience as an auditor, I always looked at life measured by how much we give and take. But when I fully surrendered myself to God, things changed. I now look at life measured by how much we give back for His kingdom. That being said, my goal in this book is to share how to live a balanced, godly life and how we can daily account for our lives to God as we journey heavenward. True-life experiences shared by friends, clients, and other people brought to me the real meaning of a God-centered life. Life application of Biblical principles validates God's existence and that His words are true and profound yesterday, today, and forever. Furthermore, the personal goal of *Accounting for Life—A Journey Heavenward* is to facilitate us in experiencing a deeper personal renewal in our relationship with God.

***Heavenly Father:***

*May the words in this book be magnified*
*As it travels far and wide.*
*May the message be carried*
*As it is purposely delivered.*
*May its journey reach out to plenty*
*As it touches the lives of many. AMEN.*

## *The Book's Mission Statement*

Through this book I hope and pray for readers:

- To get to know the Lord and find God's purpose in their lives;
- To grow in spiritual maturity in their relationship with the Lord;
- To apply principles of Biblical wisdom resulting in kingdom impact;
- To be of service to others and the church where they worship by modeling faithful stewardship of time, abilities, talents, and material treasures;
- To strengthen family relationships and lead balanced and God-centered lives;
- To pursue intimacy with God as they journey heavenward.

***Heavenly Father:***

*May the mission be the vision*
*Carried all throughout the nation*
*To know the Lord and find purpose,*
*To bring encouragement and hope,*
*To strengthen family relationships.*
*These things I pray in Jesus' wonderful name. AMEN.*

## *The Book's Concept and Insight*

In this book, the phrase, "accounting for life" or "accountable to God" is repeatedly used to represent our accountability to God for our actions, words, thoughts, and deeds. Bible verses are quoted to substantiate and support every assertion. These are God's commands, which will teach us, guide us, and direct us to find meaning and purpose for our lives.

Each chapter and section starts with wisdom and insight, guided by relevant Scriptures related to each topic. This is followed by real-life personal testimonials that will inspire us with how God has touched lives. These revelations are designed to kindle and rekindle a passion for unbroken intimacy with God.

Each chapter and section ends with a prayer and personal reflections. Readers are encouraged to reflect on the truths and principles that have been set forth and consider how these should change their outlook on life. Indeed, this book will remind us to pray and to read God's Word to reinforce us with Biblical wisdom to live out our daily walk with God as we journey heavenward.

***Heavenly Father:***

*May Your Scriptures teach, guide, and direct us.*
*May this book's concept and insight inspire and support us,*
*And may the real-life personal testimonials touch our lives,*
*Passionately testifying to the truth that You're real and alive.*
*Father, with the writing of this book,* Accounting for Life,
*May You open every reader's heart to be able to realize*
*That only in You, Almighty Father, everything will materialize*
*If we continue to rightfully seek You as we journey heavenward. AMEN.*

## *Author's Personal Commitment*

Looking back in time, I came to realize that, in order to live my life to the fullest, I must be rightly related to God. In John 15:9-11, Jesus said, "As the Father has loved me, so have I loved you. Now remain in my love. If you obey my commands, you will remain in my love, just as I have obeyed my Father's commands and remain in his love. I have told you this so that my joy may be in you and that your joy may be complete." Jesus' obedience to the Father, His complete surrender to what His Father sent Him to do, was the basis of His joy. Through His dying on the cross to redeem us from our sins, Jesus has introduced this joy to us. But I must be obedient to His commands if I am to experience the same joy. Being rightly related to God allows Him to bring out the best in me. In Psalm 31:5 is a commitment: "Into your hands I commit my spirit; redeem me, O Lord, the God of truth." I therefore commit to be accountable to God for all my actions, words, thoughts, and deeds in all facets of my life. And I commit to continually seek Him with all my heart, as stated in Deuteronomy 4:29: "But if from there you seek the Lord your God, you will find him if you look for him with all your heart and with all your soul."

If only I had kept records of all my life entries and been accountable to God, what a blessing it could have been to say, "Thanks, God; I have lived a balanced, godly life." Yet this is something I still hope to do. In fact, being faithful and obedient to Him, accentuated by my passion to share God's love for mankind, has resulted in this book.

I claim as my own the prayer in Psalm 20:4: "May He give you the desire of your heart and make all your plans succeed." It is my fervent hope and prayer that through this book, God will pave the way for all of us to say, as Paul did in Philippians 3:14, "I press on toward the goal to win the prize for which God has called me heavenward in Christ Jesus."

***Heavenly Father****, unto You I humbly commit myself*
*To be accountable for my actions, words, thoughts, and deeds,*
*To continually seek You with all my heart and with all my soul,*
*To be faithful and obedient to share Your love to mankind,*
*As I fervently hope and pray that You will pave the way*
*To a journey that leads me to kingdom authority. AMEN.*

## *Author's Personal Statement*

This book is the by-product of my passion in life, a life journey seeking God through my relationship with Him and with others.

It all started with a dream that someday I wanted to make a big difference in the lives of others. As a financial advisor, I am uniquely positioned to reach out to people, not only regarding their financial concerns, but also regarding their life problems. My services expanded beyond the call of duty so that I also became a friend, mentor, and confidante. During the process, I came across people in all walks of life with different life situations. My personality was to cling strongly to people's feelings in every financial or emotional concern they have. I could easily get attached and become compassionate toward friends, clients, and others, business and non-business associates alike. Sometimes I questioned whether this was a good thing. I prayed about it, and I went with the flow of my truthful feelings. Lo and behold, my Father in heaven always put everything into perspective.

I was drawn to the idea that, if and when opportunity comes as I meet people who needed my advice, my goal would be to try my very best to give that advice. Allowing God's interventions in all my advice would be a part of the process. Most often, people just want someone to listen to their problems and to be their friend. But sometimes they may even be looking for mentors. Sometimes they just want confirmation of whether what they are doing is right or wrong. And if I need to cry with them or pray with them, then I will. After all, I know and I am sure that my Father in heaven is by my side, as Deuteronomy 31:8 reminds us: "The Lord himself goes before you and will be with you; he will never leave you nor forsake you. Do not be afraid; do not be discouraged." I must always have faith and confidence in my Father in heaven that He will always stand with me.

Very often I tell others that God does not want us to be troubled. Presenting our requests to God will alleviate worries, as Philippians 4:6 says: "Do not be anxious about anything, but in everything, by prayer and petition, with thanksgiving, present your requests to God." Being anxious for nothing means not to worry because worry indicates a lack of trust in God's wisdom and power.

My good relationship with people exemplifies my love for the Lord, and my conviction is to make my practice His purpose for me. Ephesians 5:15-17 says, "Be very careful, then, how you live—not as unwise but as wise, making the most of every opportunity, because the days are evil. Therefore do not be foolish, but understand what the Lord's will is." To make the most of my time here on earth, fulfilling God's purpose is crucial for me. I must utilize every opportunity for useful worship and service. I thank God for giving me the wisdom and the conviction. Therefore, I must be obedient and faithful to explore more opportunities that align with God's will for me. Every morning before I get out of bed, I ask for God's wisdom and daily provisions, and through my prayer, this becomes my everyday meditation.

***Heavenly Father:***

*I give You the honor, praise, and glory*
*For today and every day I am yours.*
*Use me for Your purpose.*

*Thank You, Father, that:*
*You equipped me with tools to use and*
*Direct me to the people who need them.*
*May Your will be done in me, upon me, and through me.*
*I submit myself to You.*
*Make me the person You want me to be,*
*As I humbly say:*
*With you, I am able, willing, and ready.*
*I ask these things in Jesus' mighty name. AMEN.*

God answers prayer. Jesus said in Matthew 7:7, "Ask and it will be given to you, seek and you will find, knock and the door will be opened to you." Never did it occur to me that I would be teaching a Bible study, but I ended up having to teach one. It was a step of faith for me. When I was planning to start the study, my husband asked me, "What do you think you're doing?" I was very confident with my answer to him: "I don't know, but I am sure that this is what I must do."

Teaching the businesswomen's Bible study was a great blessing. It gave me the confidence to embrace new dimensions in life. Serving the Lord in this capacity made the greatest transformation in my life. Every night as I was spending hours preparing for my next Bible study lessons, I put my trust in the Lord to direct and guide me. Being faithful and obedient to studying His words enhanced my yearning for Him. I thank God for providing me the spirit of wisdom and revelation so that I might know Him better through the process. The more I focused on God's Word, the more it was manifested in my heart and in my daily walk with Him, and this gave me the audacity to reach out more to people for kingdom priority.

God's promise in Jeremiah 29:11-13 highlighted my passion to serve Him more: "'For I know I have plans for you,' declares the Lord, 'plans to prosper you and not to harm you, plans to give you hope and a future. Then you will call upon me and come and pray to me, and I will listen to you. You will seek me and find me when you seek me with all your heart.'" The recent economic uncertainty brought worries to many, including a lot of my friends and clients. There was a lot of negative impact on all of us. Mostly, the decline in housing value, the stock market decline, and the loss of jobs were our big concerns. All that I could share with people was to trust in the Lord. Nahum 1:7 says, "The Lord is good, a refuge in times of trouble. He cares for those who trust in him."

I really believe that these crises were driven by many people's personal greed. Every day that I encounter people with these kinds of problems, the more I am drawn to asking God, "What can I do?" Is this book the answer to my question? Only God knows. So let us start our journey together!

***

*Chapter One*

# WHO AM I TO GOD?

Who am I to God? This question goes to the very core of our existence. Apart from God, we are nothing. Indeed, in Isaiah 45:5, the Lord says, "I am the Lord, and there is no other; apart from me there is no God. I will strengthen you, though you have not acknowledged me." The following Scriptures relate to God's creation and ownership of us.

> The earth is the Lord's, and everything in it, the world, and all who live in it. (Psalm 24:1)

> Through him all things were made; without him nothing was made that has been made. (John 1:3)

> Wealth and honor come from you; you are the ruler of all things. In your hands are strength and power to exalt and give strength to all. (1 Chronicles 29:12)

In Isaiah 43:7, the Lord speaks of "everyone who is called by my name, whom I created for my glory, whom I formed and made." God created us for the purpose of glorifying Him. Therefore, acknowledging and believing God's creation and ownership of us will allow us to accomplish His planned purpose.

God owns everything. He is the Master of all. We are His creation, and He knows what's going on in us. With His power and His provision, we must trust in Him. Because God is our true owner, we have responsibilities. Because God loves us so much, He created us above all His other creations on earth and to rule over them. God gave us a mind, body, and soul to care for the rest of His creation. In short, we are His managers; we are His stewards. As His stewards, how then can we account for everything that was entrusted to us by God?

If every day we had to account for all of these things, it would be insurmountable. We would just be spending our time collecting and recollecting what had occurred. This would be impossible considering that we have our own lives to live, lives we share with others (families, friends, colleagues, and our work). For this reason, God gave us commands to live by, not by might nor by power, but by His Word.

The Word of the Lord operates like a compass that controls all facets of our lives, the spiritual, financial, emotional, and physical. God's Word gives direction to our lives. In our spiritual lives, it is reflected by our faith. As Hebrews 11:3 says, "By faith we understand that the universe was formed at God's command, so that what is seen was not made out of what was visible." Also, Hebrews 11:1 says, "Now faith is being sure of what we hope for and certain of what we do not see." In our financial lives, we know that God owns everything. We are just God's stewards of our material resources. The words we tell ourselves in our minds have the power to change our behavior; therefore, we have to guard our minds from the corrupting influence of our environment. We must take care of our bodies because 1 Corinthians 6:19 says, "Do you not know that your body is a temple of the Holy Spirit, who is in you, whom you have received from God? You are not your own." A Christian's body belongs to the Lord.

As I was growing up, I was always told to go to school, finish well, and earn money. This was the way to survive in life. I was never told that God loves me and has a plan for me, as I was told when I received the Lord as my personal Savior. Everything that happened in my childhood until I came to know the Lord was focused on chasing after earthly, material possessions. I did well in school, earned my degree, got a job, and then got married. Although I graduated from a religious school, who would think that all I remembered learning was that God created me, that I must live a life always believing that God is watching over me, and that I must be a good person. Honestly, I became the person I believed I should be in God's eyes, only to realize that it was not through my good works that I could be saved but only through Jesus. Everyone must know that only through Jesus we come to know God; it is not through our good works. Ephesians 2:8-9 says, "For it is by grace you have been saved, through faith—and this not from yourselves, it is a gift of God—not by works, so that no one can boast." It is not through our works but by God's grace through our faith that we have been saved. This is the basis on which we can grow in our relationship with God. Thus, blessing comes from God on the basis of our faith. Therefore, having been saved and given a new identity, we are redefined as new creations. With our new spiritual position as a new creation, God empowers us to do all the things we can do, and we enjoy life through our faith in Christ. Now that we walk in the Spirit, we certainly can proclaim what Jesus said in Matthew 22:37: "Love the Lord your God with all your heart and with all your soul and with all your mind."

I knew nothing about true salvation or about God owning everything until I received the Lord as my Savior. Then, seeking Him and asking Him to provide me the spirit of wisdom and the revelation to know Him more paved the way to kingdom opportunity. In Philippians 2:13, we are told, "For it is God who works in you to will and to act according to his good purpose." Although we are responsible to work, it is God who actually produces the good work in us. Our desires and actions fulfill God's purpose as we are energized by God and continue to abide in His love.

***Heavenly Father**:*

*Who am I to You, Father? Only You would know.*
*But seeking You in my life You began to show.*

*Being obedient to Your words I began to grow.*

*When I fully surrender my life unto You,*
*As I worship, honor, and adore You,*
*Then you bring truth to who I am to You.*

*With all your wonderful provision,*
*Father, You created me for a reason,*
*And that is to glorify You all season. AMEN.*

***Personal Reflection (Who Am I to God?):***

- Describe your earliest recollection of your introduction to God and Christianity.
- Personalize your answer to this question: Who am I to God?
- How dependent are you on God's provision? How does His Word impact all facets of your life (spiritual, financial, emotional, and physical)?
- What is your perspective regarding God as the owner of everything?
- Write your personal prayer.

## *The Gift of Salvation: An Invitation*

The Lord is my strength and my song; he has become my salvation. He is my God, and I will praise him, my father's God, and I will exalt him. (Exodus 15:2)

It is very important to know that we all have direct access to the Father through the Son. This direct access to God comes through the gift of salvation. God's gracious gift of salvation is freely available to whoever believes in Christ. Before we can be rightly related to God, it is necessary to understand and acknowledge what God has done for us and to know what we must do. There are four basic spiritual laws a person has to know and believe as a Christian.

***First,*** we must know God's position—that *God is holy, and God loves us*. We know that God is a holy God, but He loves us and has a plan for us. John 3:16 says, "For God so loved the world that he gave his one and only Son, that whoever believes in him shall not perish but have **eternal life**." And John 17:3 says, "Now this is **eternal life**: that they may know you, the only true God, and Jesus Christ, whom you have sent." God's love for us was supremely demonstrated by sending His beloved Son to die on our behalf while we were yet sinners.

***Second,*** we must know man's condition—that *man is sinful*. I refer here to what we call original sin and personal sin. Original sin refers to the sin of Adam, while personal sins are the sins we individually commit. Adam's sin was placed on man's account as stated in Romans 5:12-13: "Therefore, just as sin entered the world through one man, and death through sin, and in this way death came to all men, because all sinned—for before the law was given, sin was in the world."

In Romans 6:23, Paul says, "For the wages of sin is death, but the gift of God is **eternal life** in Christ Jesus our Lord." Death in this Scripture refers to spiritual death while eternal life refers to everlasting life, without end. Spiritual death is the penalty for our slavery to sin, and eternal life is a free gift from God for believing in Him.

***Third,*** we need to know God's provision—that *Christ died for us*. First and foremost, we have to understand that there is an infinite gulf between holy God and a sinful person, precluding us from knowing God personally. Although we may continually reach out to God through our good works, good character, and personal effort in hope of establishing a personal relationship with Him, we fail. Why? Because in John 14:6, Jesus said, "I am the way, and the truth, and the life. No one comes to the Father, except through me." Therefore, only through Jesus, not through our good works, do we come to know God. It is said in Romans

5:8, "But God demonstrates His own love for us in this: While we were still sinners, Christ died for us." God's unconditional love bridged the gulf between holy God and sinful man through the death of Jesus Christ. Jesus died to reconcile us to a holy God who was alienated from us because of our sin. He died on the cross to ransom us from the penalty of sin. Now that we know the consequences of the original sin, what then shall we do?

***Fourth,*** we must understand man's decision—that *man must receive Jesus Christ as Savior and Lord.* Because of God's gracious gift of salvation, bridging the gulf between holy God and sinful man through the death of Jesus Christ, we can receive Jesus as our Lord and Savior. In 1 Thessalonians 5:9, we are told, "For God did not appoint us to suffer wrath but to receive salvation through our Lord Jesus Christ."

The book of Ephesians (2:8-9) states, "For it is by grace you have been saved, through faith—and this not from yourselves, it is the gift of God—not by works, so that no one can boast." God's grace offers pardon for our sin. Grace in Christian theology is the free and unmerited favor of God. God's grace is manifested in the salvation of sinners. Salvation is a blessing for believers, but even more than that, it glorifies God to bestow His endless grace. If salvation is by God's grace, then we must simply, through faith, receive Jesus Christ as our personal Lord and Savior.

Revelation 3:20 says, "Here I am! I stand at the door and knock. If anyone hears my voice and opens the door, I will come in and eat with him, and he with me." This Scripture is an invitation from God that when we receive Christ, we experience a new birth. New birth refers to a spiritual birth that allows you to become a new creation.

Congratulations, you have just learned the four spiritual laws. Your journey of joy heavenward starts by praying this prayer.

## *Prayer of Salvation*

*Lord Jesus, I am a sinner, and I'm sorry for all of my sins. Please forgive me.*
*I thank You for dying on the cross for my sins.*
*I open the door of my heart, and I ask You to come into my life,*
*To be my personal Savior and my Lord.*
*Take control of the throne of my life.*
*Make me the kind of person You want me to be*
*That I may receive the gift of eternal life. AMEN.*

If you have prayed this prayer of salvation with true conviction in your heart, you are now a follower of Jesus. This is now the start of a new beginning in a personal relationship with God. Your aim should be to have spiritual fullness in Christ as indicated in Colossians 2:6: "So then, just as you received Christ Jesus as Lord, continue to live in him." It is with fervent hope and prayer that you will be encouraged to grow in the knowledge of God through His Word, the Bible.

***Personal Reflection (The Gift of Salvation)**:*

- Did someone share God's love and plan with you?
- Knowing that you have direct access to God's gift of salvation, are you now ready to receive this gracious gift?
- Pray the prayer of salvation.
- Become familiar with the four spiritual laws; study and meditate on them.
- Start sharing the gift of salvation with others.
- Write your personal prayer.

## *Personal Encounter with the Lord*

The year was 1997 when I received the Lord as my Savior. I was at the lowest point of my married life. I was very vulnerable. My husband and I were having marital problems after he admitted that he had an affair with another woman. I was saddened and shocked, but even more, I was intrigued when he claimed that he was being tempted. James 1:14 says, "But each one is tempted when, by his own evil desire, he is dragged away and enticed." No one should say he is innocent in being tempted. In reality, he is being deceived by his own evil desire.

This marital problem seemed unbearable, especially knowing that my husband broke one of the Ten Commandments, "You shall not commit adultery" (Exodus 20:14). It was indeed a very hard and long healing process for me. Part of the healing process was claiming the promise in James 1:12: "Blessed is the man who perseveres under trial, because when he has stood the test, he will receive the crown of life that God has promised to those who love him."

Although this experience brought the greatest trial of my life, I could also consider this to be the most significant turning point in my entire life. In Romans 12:2, it is strongly said, "Do not conform any longer to the pattern of this world but be transformed by the renewing of your mind. Then you will be able to test and approve what God's will is—his good, pleasing and perfect will." Receiving God's greatest gift of salvation gave me instant hope and encouragement. I looked at this particular experience as affirmation of my relationship with God. We live in an imperfect world, and God allows imperfect things to happen to us to test our faithfulness. Sometimes we persevere through our trials and realize, as James 1:3 says, that "the testing of your faith develops perseverance." Had I not encountered this traumatic experience, I might not have had the opportunity to know and to receive the Lord. I will forever be thankful and grateful to Pastor Mendoza and to my dear friends and neighbors, Mr. and Mrs. E. Cueva, who love the Lord so much. They shared with me the love of the Lord and introduced me to my Savior.

In 2007, my best friend Carmen died of an aneurysm. Death is inevitable, but her death devastated me. I had to take six months' leave from work to be relieved of the pain of losing a dear friend. Part of the resentment was that I missed the opportunity to share the love of the Lord with her and to see her receive the gift of salvation. Following is a poem that I wrote in memory of my best friend, Carmen Campos, who was always there for me. This is an excerpt of the eulogy I gave at her funeral. I wrote this to describe who Carmen was to me and to everyone she loved.

## CARMEN

***C***- *Caring for all her friends she loved*
***A***- *Always and ever all the day of her life*
***R***- *Remembering and reminding all of their tasks*
***M***- *Memories of her will surely last*
***E***- *Eternally and forever she will be loved*
***N***- *Never did I expect life for her to go this fast*

The following year, Agnes, another friend and a client, was diagnosed with lung cancer. God led me to reach out to her, pray for her, and spend time with her. Praise God! I was able to witness to her and share with her the love of the Lord. She received the Lord, and to the last days of her life, I felt her love for Him. After her death, her beloved husband shared with me the amazing changes he felt at his wife's deathbed. He said, "She died very peacefully." It was at that moment that I knew she had gone home to be with the Lord. Praise God!

Incredibly, it did not end there; two months later, Lychia, another dear friend, died. She was also my client and a former coworker. We had worked together for many years, and I knew her very well. Before her death, she had become very resentful and frustrated because she couldn't find a job after she was terminated by her last employer. It came as a shock to me when I heard that she had died. I was in a state of disbelief.

While I was attending to the financial matters of these two dear friends, I was also grieving for their families. It was a big challenge for my career to encounter such an ordeal. But I held on tight to God's promise in Psalm 9:10: "Those who know your name will trust in you, for you, Lord, have never forsaken those who seek you."

The decline in the market brought significant changes to my clients' portfolios, and this didn't make things easy for me either. But God's guidance and direction of my portfolio choices for them led me to a less volatile positioning.

Both God's fulfilled and as-yet unfulfilled promises in my life brought significant meaning and purpose. They contributed to amazing transformations in my life and in the lives of my family and friends. Regardless of the situation, we must be dependent upon God's promises at all times. At first, intimacy with God came mostly during my trials. But now, being intimate with God at all times gives me the passion to share God's love with many people. God's amazing grace and mercy to mankind has created in me the power to forgive and the power to love just as God loves us. In 2 Peter 1:3, we read, "His divine power has given us everything we need for life and godliness through our knowledge of him who called us by his own glory and goodness."

***Heavenly Father*:**

*Right around the time before I found You, I was so vulnerable,*
*Having a marital problem that seemed so unbearable.*
*Though this experience brought trial and tribulation into my life,*

*Significantly it became the greatest turning point in my whole life.*

*My Father in Heaven:*
*Unto You I pray and thank You*
*For opening the door to my heart*
*To come to know You and honor You*
*To be my Lord and Savior.*
*Help me to not let loose of my grip upon Your promises,*
*For they are the stronghold in my challenges.*
*They give me guidance and direction as I speak*
*Of my heavenly faith and hope in You, Lord. AMEN.*

***Personal Reflection (Personal Encounter with the Lord)***:

- Describe your personal encounter with the Lord.
- What was the significance of your personal encounter with the Lord?
- Were there people who significantly impacted and spiritually touched you, or vice versa?
- Write your testimony of this encounter.
- Write your personal prayer.

## *The Fear of the Lord*

The following Scriptures relating to the fear of the Lord promote deeper spiritual intimacy with God.

> The fear of the Lord is the beginning of knowledge, but fools despise wisdom and discipline. (Proverbs 1:7)

God is holy, majestic, and magnificent. He possesses great power, honor, and glory, so we must revere Him. Reverence for God is the foundation for all spiritual knowledge and wisdom.

> My son, if you accept my words and store up my commands within you, turning your ear to wisdom and applying your heart to understanding, and if you call out for insight and cry aloud for understanding, and if you look for it as for silver and search for it as for hidden treasure, then you will understand the fear of the Lord and find the knowledge of God. For the Lord gives wisdom, and from his mouth come knowledge and understanding. (Proverbs 2:1-6)

Wisdom has the power to transform life; it comes from within and leads to a change outside. Wisdom implies knowledge and understanding of what is right, just, and fair.

> The fear of the Lord teaches a man wisdom, and humility comes before honor. (Proverbs 15:33)

> Let all the earth fear the Lord; let all the people of the world revere him. (Psalm 33:8)

> To fear the Lord is to hate evil; I hate pride and arrogance, evil behavior and perverse speech. (Proverbs 8:13)

> The fear of the Lord adds length to life, but the years of the wicked are cut short. (Proverbs 10:27)

> Better a little with the fear of the Lord than great wealth with turmoil. (Proverbs 15:16)

> The fear of the Lord is a fountain of life, turning a person from the snares of death. (Proverbs 14:27)

> Humility is the fear of the Lord; its wages are riches and honor and life. (Proverbs 22:4)

Do not let your heart envy sinners, but always be zealous for the fear of the Lord. (Proverbs 23:17)

One afternoon I was on the phone with a friend, sharing my faith and love for the Lord. It was a very pleasant conversation because we were both acknowledging God's provisions and blessings to us and thanking Him for them. Somehow during our conversation, I started sharing from the book of Proverbs, and I quoted Proverbs 1:7: "The fear of the Lord is the beginning of knowledge..." I didn't know how she would react to the concept, but she began to comment, "Why should I fear the Lord? Must I not love Him instead of being fearful of Him?" Sometimes the phrase, "the fear of the Lord," can easily be misunderstood. The fear of the Lord means to be in reverence of God because He is majestic, holy, and magnificent.

Through the fear of the Lord we learn to honor, respect, and glorify God. We therefore demonstrate a true submission to God and His Word. As we journey together seeking God, we begin to understand the meaning of the phrase, "fear of the Lord" and how we can apply its benefits to our spiritual intimacy with Him.

***Heavenly Father**:*

*Great power, honor, and glory are Yours.*
*Please teach us to truly demonstrate our reverence for You*
*As we continually seek You for Your kingdom authority.*
*Lead us to a journey pursuing intimacy with You, God Almighty. AMEN.*

***Personal Reflection (The Fear of the Lord)**:*

- Describe your understanding of the fear of the Lord.
- How does the phrase, "fear of the Lord" impact your personal relationship with God?

- Write of any significant experience that demonstrates your fear of the Lord.
- Write your personal prayer.

## *Every Day Is a New Beginning*

Lamentations 3:22-23 says, "Because of the Lord's great love we are not consumed, for his compassions never fail. They are new every morning; great is your faithfulness." God created each day differently. Yesterday is gone, never to come back; today is here to enjoy and make the best of; and tomorrow is yet to come, and offers us the chance to explore new things. Jesus said in Matthew 6:34, "Therefore, do not worry about tomorrow, for tomorrow will worry about itself. Each day has enough trouble of its own." Each new day, God gives us opportunity for a new beginning to come to Him and build our personal relationship with Him. I believe this is part of God's plan for us. God, in His mighty power and love, gives us opportunities each day to make a difference in our lives and in the lives of others. Every day that He creates is never to be wasted. Let us rejoice and be glad in it.

When I first received the Lord, I was clueless to which direction I was heading. All I was sure about was that God loved me. He was just to forgive my sins and relieve my pain and suffering. Little did I know that my personal relationship with Him would blossom. However, it was a very long process of transformation. At first, I was just attending church services, then I started going to Bible studies. It was not too long before I began to notice a positive outlook on life. Since it was just my two daughters and I living at our house during those times, I made my home available for a lot of church functions. I even made sure that my two daughters also were involved in the church activities.

My husband then was staying with my mother and my sister in Guam. This was part of the agreement between my husband and me to give me space to recover from my pain. Somehow the arrangement worked well, and he managed to stay and work in Guam for over two years. As I was working and attending to my children, who were both in high school, I continued to get actively involved with the church activities. Reading the Bible also became my daily routine. I hoped that it would make my pain go away. That was not completely the case, but it surely helped. For the most part, I think, I just covered up the pain by redirecting my focus to a different arena of my personal goals.

When my husband decided to come back home to us, our relationship seemed better, but my pain lingered on. I constantly dwelt on what happened in the past. The worst part was that I still felt that his side of the family was against me. The thought that they were accessories to the whole ordeal continued to haunt me. What's even more intriguing was that I felt that his side of the family really didn't care about our relationship, especially after we got back together. Every time that I was triggered by my emotional condition, I reacted bitterly. Building my personal relationship with God was a constant struggle. I felt like the more I reached out to God, the more I lost confidence in my husband's truthfulness. There was always the feeling of distrust, even though I knew the Lord—or did I?

Although I was still suffering from the trauma, I never let go of my career goals and the goals for my daughters' education. These were my top priorities during those years. My two daughters continued to excel in school; I enrolled in a master's program. Fourteen months later, I successfully graduated with a Master's Degree in Financial Management. That same year, my younger daughter also graduated from high school. On top of all these obligations, I was also working part-time for another company. I was therefore going to school, working full-time and part-time, not to mention being a full-time mother of two teenagers. I guess my strong-willed personality helped me survive. But as I think of it now, that was a time of God's intervention in my life. In spite of my busy schedule, I still found time to pray and read the Bible, day in and day out. I never stopped yearning for God's presence in my life. But during those years, there seemed to be a missing piece of the puzzle that I cannot connect to the reality of life.

After I graduated from my masters program, God led me to a totally different career path. I became a financial advisor. It was not a big transition for me because I knew that I was well prepared for this profession, considering my educational background and my thesis on financial planning. In fact, it gave me the most rewarding and fulfilling career ever. I always knew that it was part of God's plan for me.

In the meantime, my relationship with my husband didn't seem to get any better. But there was one thing that was very reassuring—our disagreements lessened. As always, I continued to escape from the reality of the problem by diverting my attention again and again to other things. What worried me the most, though, was the recurring emotional pain.

Long before all those years that I was suffering from my husband's infidelity, I was already constantly receiving harassing letters. Over a period of ten years, those letters continually arrived. I lost track of how many of them came in the mail, but it was nerve-racking to even open my mailbox. The letters were very disturbing, and they all came from an anonymous person. I was in a constant fear of people around me. The contents of these letters were very graphic, malicious, wicked, and demeaning. I made several attempts to report these to the police, but I was told that there was not much they could do until I had a suspect. What scared me the most was that at times I also received scary phone messages saying, "I will kill you." I strongly believe that whoever was doing this purposely intended to ruin my family relationships. This time I was sure it did not have anything to do with my husband's past extramarital affair. This was an isolated case, I thought. I pretended to ignore the matter. I just asked my church elders or my pastor to pray for me to be relieved of the pain and suffering.

Still, the harassing letters continued to arrive, and soon the messages were conveyed to my younger daughter, Karina. At her school dorm, she received a four-page summary of all the harassing letters that had been sent to me. Unaware of my situation, she was in state of shock after reading all those demeaning, malicious, and slandering words. She cried a lot, fearful of my safety and hers. As a mother, there's nothing more devastating than seeing your daughter get hurt. I was so worried for her safety that I was convinced to even further pursue the matter in the courts. After seeking help from the authorities and my church elders, I took their advice to just let it go. I began to pray for this person, whoever he or she was. I had a lot of explaining to do with my daughter and hoped she understood everything. I praised God for His guidance and protection for my daughter because she recovered quickly.

Every day I continued to pray to God, asking Him what to do and begging Him to put an end to all my pain and suffering. On a few occasions, I wished I would never again wake up in the morning, and I even thought of relocating to a different state, away from all this trouble. As I was suffering, I could also feel my husband's pain. He was very sorry and felt very regretful for what he did, and he often said, "I wish it had never happened." Over time, I began to encounter health problems and had to undergo surgery. I believed that such was caused by my prolonged emotional self-pity, discouragement, and disappointments. I had several problems that were diagnosed as having been caused by my unstable emotional condition. I felt like I was pushing myself to the edge. "I've had enough of this," I thought. There were days and nights of pure agony. "Why me, Lord, I cried? What have I done to deserve all of this?" I was in search of an answer and in need of healing.

My relationship with my in-laws continued to bother me, and I put a stop to my communication with them. I tried to stay away from them, hoping to bring closure to my relationship with them. Our family drama, not to mention the accumulated harassment that I received for over a decade, brought more pain and suffering. I felt that my emotional energy was being consumed for the wrong purpose. Dwelling on who hurt me aggravated further my health problems. But I never stopped seeking the Lord's direction and guidance. Family and friends continued to pray for me and tell me to let go of any distractions. But "forgetting what is behind and straining toward what is ahead" (Philippians 3:13) was never meant to be my complete healing process. In fact, it took another six years of all these things continuing to happen.

Looking back on all those years of pain, suffering, and constant arguing with my husband and his family, I came to realize how it was really damaging my health, and especially my family. I was determined to put an end to all of this, but the question was, "How?" Then one day it happened: God answered all my prayers. He revealed to me the virtue of forgiveness. Matthew 6:12 says, "Forgive us our debts, as we also have forgiven our debtors." It was at Christmastime when God revealed to me, through the reading of His Word, the power of forgiveness. God's command regarding forgiveness was the missing piece of the puzzle for me to be able to move on and to reconnect my life to the real world. Forgiveness requires humility, as described in Philippians 2:3: "Do nothing out of selfish ambition or vain conceit. Rather, in *humility* consider others better than yourselves." God's Word opened my heart to a real and godly perspective. Amazingly enough, I learned to let go of the past; and from then on, I no longer received the harassing letters and nobody ever bothered us again. I thanked God for another answered prayer.

Each day that God created is an opportunity to come to know Him, to ask forgiveness, and to start a personal relationship with Him. Therefore, every day is a new beginning. With that, I began to slowly forgive all those who had wronged me. The biggest transformation of my life came when I turned fifty years old and I rededicated my life to Jesus to use me for His purpose. My husband came to follow Jesus a few years later, after he realized the good things God was doing in our lives. God's awesomeness shall I proclaim!

***Heavenly Father:***

*Every day that You've created is an opportunity*
*To make a difference in our lives and in the lives of many and*
*To establish a personal relationship with God Almighty.*

*Yesterday is gone, never to come back.*
*Today we must enjoy and make the best of it,*
*For tomorrow will have its own worries.*

*Thanks be to God that every day is a new beginning. AMEN.*

***Personal Reflection (Every Day Is a New Beginning):***

- What significance does each day bring to your relationship with the Lord?
- What changes and opportunities await you each day that God created?
- What opportunities will you take advantage of for God's kingdom?
- Write your personal prayer.

## *Vision for Life*

In 2 Corinthians 4:16-18 it is said, "Therefore, we do not lose heart. Though outwardly we are wasting away, yet inwardly we are being renewed day by day. For our light and momentary troubles are achieving for us an eternal glory that far outweighs them all. So we fix our eyes not on what is seen, but on what is unseen. For what is seen is temporary, but what is unseen is eternal."

In our lives we experience adversity, affliction, doubts, and tremendous pain and suffering. In the midst of all these experiences that we go through, God says not to lose heart, for these are temporary. In Romans 8:18, Paul says, "I consider that our present sufferings are not worth comparing with the glory that will be revealed in us." What awaits us in God's future is glory; therefore, we need to focus our lives on things that are eternal.

God has a purpose for all of us. Relative to that purpose, it is important to know that God is preparing His vision for us. This vision is what we need to embrace, for in doing so we can withstand difficulty, uncertainty, and hardship with our unwavering faith in God. It is essential to be spiritual in our vision for life, understanding where we're coming from, why we're here, and where we're going. To live as a person of vision is to be aware of the presence of God in our everyday lives and to understand that we need to pursue God's calling and purpose in our lives. God knows the focus of our hearts. As we begin to respond to His calling, we first must determine our visionary concept and align it with God's perspectives. Second, we need to identify our God-driven purpose (worship, fellowship, ministry, discipleship). Besides making Himself known to us, God wants us to have a clearer image of the work we need to do and our arena of influence for His kingdom.

I began to embrace God's vision for my life during the course of my emotional pain and suffering over a long period of time. God's vision for my life came to me in a very slow process as I continually sought God. Gradually, my lifestyle changed as I pursued the things of God, daily asking Him to give me a clearer vision of His purpose for me. I've dealt with numerous challenges during the process, including persecution, but almost always I have continued to persevere, for God is my stable rock.

Heaven is home for believers and all we hope for is a permanent reward in heaven. In the meantime, are we focusing on the things of God? Are we in total submission to Him? Is God our stronghold and the center of our lives? Do we declare Him to be important? Remember that God's vision for our lives will be revealed through our hearts as we journey heavenward to His kingdom and as we continue to pursue His purpose. Keep asking yourself, "What is the deepest longing of my heart? Am I seeking God's illuminating vision to light my paths?"

***Heavenly Father:***

*As I meditate day and night I bring You my plea.*
*Reveal in me a clearer vision of Your purpose*
*That I may know the things You want me to achieve.*
*Allow me to see the things You declare important*
*That I may feel the deepest longing of my heart*
*As I journey heavenward to Your kingdom's glory. AMEN.*

***Personal Reflection (Vision for Life):***

- Assess the things that you declare are important to you.
- Have you had any particular experience that affirms your relationship with God?
- Are there circumstances in your life that God has used to minister to people?
- Ask God to give you a clearer image of the work you need to do for His purpose.
- What is your vision for life? Is your vision one God has prepared you for?
- What is the deepest longing of your heart?
- Write your personal prayer.

## *Living with Passion*

Each of us has a passion for something, but not everyone gets the chance to discover it. I never even realized what my passion was until I came to America, went back to school, and discovered for myself what I really wanted to do. In my culture, children are taught to be obedient to their parents, and part of their obedience is submitting to their parents' plan for them. The chances are slim to none that children will be able to choose what they want to do in life, and it is even less likely they will be able to pursue their passion. This is because resources are very limited and because parents expect so much from their children in helping with the family finances and especially in helping finance their siblings' education. This greatly limits what children can do.

Passion is a lifelong commitment to the things that matter most to us. It comes from our deepest longing, ignited and reignited from the fired-up desire of our heart. One can be passionate about many different things. It is my conviction, however, that our passion must be for the things of God that will nurture and empower us to exemplify our God-given talents or abilities for His glory. There are ways and means to access God's provision for the purpose of glorifying Him. *First*, on a personal level, God provided for us our career. Are we passionate about disseminating our services through our career? Are we incorporating God as a partner in accomplishing our goal to service or help others? Are there other people benefiting from what we do? Are we glorifying God with what we do? *Second*, on a relationship level, God wants us to love one another. Are we passionate about our relationships with our spouse, our children, and others? Is our ultimate passion to serve the Lord? If so, hold on tight, because the evil one could snatch it away from you.

You have to understand that your passion could be at stake at some point in your life due to health problems, emotional problems, relationship problems, and financial problems. Always be on guard, and have your full trust in God. Everything that works for and against you is a part of the process. It is like a cycle that brings you to high and low moments. Remember, we are still on our journey. We are not home yet, and until we arrive, we have to stand firm. As Ephesians 6:12-14 says,

> For our struggle is not against flesh and blood, but against the rulers, against the authorities, against the powers of this dark world and against the spiritual forces of evil in the heavenly realms. Therefore put on the full armor of God, so that when the day of evil comes, you may be able to stand your ground, and after you have done everything, to stand. Stand firm then, with the belt of truth buckled around your waist, with the breastplate of righteousness in place.

At my place of work, my manager often uses me as an example of being passionate about my job. I know that I love what I do and I put my effort, time, and dedication toward it. As a financial advisor, helping people in their financial situation is my business, but having a genuine compassion for people's situations (financial and personal), I become more than their business ally. I am uniquely positioned because my clients not only entrust me with their financial decision making but also with their life planning. Finances is a very sensitive issue for people, and having access to this information prompts trust, which enables them to openly discuss their personal problems as well. I always thought that having the privilege of helping these clients in both situations is a blessing. It overwhelmed me at first, and that's how I came to realize I needed guidance from the Lord even more. Gradually, I shared my faith and love for the Lord with many people, prayed with them, and sometimes cried with them. It became a passion to me to help people in any manner God allowed. It did not stop there, though, because the more I sought God in my life, the more opportunities came to explore His kingdom authority. Teaching a businesswomen's Bible study was indeed a blessing from God; witnessing to people gave more meaning to my purpose; and now, writing this book has given life to finding the true purpose of God in my life. My compassion for people became my passion for Jesus Christ.

It is my fervent prayer that our passion for living would come from our passion for Jesus Christ, who suffered, died, was buried, and rose again for our salvation. If we know Jesus, we should have an enthusiasm and zeal for living each day.

***Heavenly Father:***

*The day I came to know You was just the beginning*
*Of something new that I look forward to every morning.*
*There were days that I didn't know what to do,*
*But You were always there to remind me of You.*

*Then one day came a new vision for me to explore,*
*Helping people with their financial situation and more.*
*My compassion became a passion for everyday living.*
*Again, Lord, You added more reasons worth believing.*

*That helping just my clients was not the end*
*But teaching Bible study could gain a friend,*
*Witnessing to people about Your love, mercy, and grace,*
*That You suffered, died on the cross for us to be saved.*

*My Lord and Savior, as Your purpose has unfolded,*
*Through the writing of this book it should be told*
*That people must account for their life as they journey heavenward,*
*For Yours is the kingdom, the power, and glory to the whole wide world. AMEN.*

***Personal Reflection (Living with Passion):***

- Do you have a passion? Describe your passion.
- Are you incorporating God as your partner to accomplish your passion?
- Are there other people benefiting from what you do? Are you glorifying God with what you do?
- Are you passionate about your relationship with your spouse, your children, and others?
- Is your ultimate passion to serve the Lord?
- Write your personal prayer.

***

# *Chapter Two*

# BUILDING RELATIONSHIPS

> Any kingdom divided against itself will be ruined and a house divided against itself will fall. (Luke 11:17)

## *Personal Relationship with God: "Synergy between God and Man"*

A journey heavenward requires a deeper and intimate spiritual relationship with God. When we enter into a relationship with God, there must be openness and no hidden secrets. Being open with God is another way of saying that we truly trust Him. We must submit ourselves to God as James 4:7 and 10 tell us: "Submit yourselves, then, to God. Resist the devil, and he will flee from you. . . . Humble yourselves before the Lord, and he will lift you up."

Where you go, what you do, and with whom you do them should reflect your total allegiance to God. Is your heart for the things of the world or for God? Only you can know where your heart leads you. Jesus said in Matthew 6:24, "No one can serve two masters. Either he will hate the one and love the other, or he will be devoted to the one and despise the other. You cannot serve both God and money." Who, then, should we serve? Unequivocally, we are to serve only God.

Building your personal relationship with God is a process. It is much like building your relationship with your spouse. My relationship with my husband was not all that dandy after his extramarital affair. It was a struggle just to keep the relationship going. My choices then were either to leave him in order to save us both from additional headaches or to keep the relationship and work things out. Somehow our love for each other kept us together, but it didn't necessarily mean life was immediately better. It took many more years to rebuild the betrayed trust. But God, in His time, miraculously healed me.

After receiving the Lord as my Savior, I began to seek God more in my life. My attitude toward life begins with my attitude toward God and how I perceive and understand Him. Thus far, the following four-step process has allowed me to properly perceive and understand Him. It also has enhanced my growth in spiritual maturity with the Lord. The four steps are: studying His Word, prayer, fellowship, and discipleship.

***The first step is studying His Word***. Believing and obeying the Word is how God's message is manifested in and through us. Proverbs 20:12 tells us, "Ears that hear and eyes that see—the Lord has made them both." The purpose of God's Word is to transform us from the inside out; however, it is also imperative that we truly respond from the heart. But before we encounter such spiritual transformation, we must study and meditate on God's Word and act according to what He has written. By faith, we know Him and believe in Him from our innermost being. Once we know Him, believe in Him, and act according to His will, we encounter spiritual transformation. We then feel the Spirit of God working within us, like our blood flowing in our human body and giving us life. Studying and meditating on the Word of God is what guides us and infuses us with the power of the Spirit of God. God's Word is like our heart, which pumps the blood through our body. Our actions truly reveal what we believe. Being obedient to God's Word depends on our desire and interest to do His will and purpose for us. Our belief, behavior, and response to His Word will reveal our true relationship with God. It is a step of faith to act in accordance with God's will and purpose for our lives. As Psalm 119:105 says, "Your word is a lamp to my feet and a light for my path."

***The second step is prayer.*** Prayer is conversation with God. Through our prayers, we make known to God ourselves, our worries, and our concern. In 2 Chronicles 6:40, Solomon prayed, "Now, my God, may your eyes be open and your ears attentive to the prayers offered in this place." God answers prayers if we trust in Him. Ezra 8:23 says, "So we fasted and petitioned our God about this, and he answered our prayer." God answers prayers because we ask with the right motives and in accordance with His will. I cannot fathom how God, in so many ways, answers my prayers.

It was a step of faith for me to write this book. For a long time, it has been the desire of my heart to write a book, but the question was how? Honestly, I don't know how to write eloquently. I always thought that for someone to be able to write a book, he or she must have a natural gift. About two years ago, I tried to enroll myself in a book writing class, but I quickly dropped out of the class after realizing it was hard for me. I shared with my classmates that I didn't belong there. It took me a while to get into the idea of writing again. This time, however, it was not even planned. It all started with my fervent prayer of how I can help others. I have always had the passion to make a difference in the lives of others, and I tried in several ways to enhance this passion. I became a member of a lot of organizations, both secular and Christian. I was a member of the board for the friends of a local library and was involved in an Asian coalition group and other community organizations. I also was inspired to charter a Lions Club known as the San Diego Premier Lions Club. I became the charter president of the club. Above all of these, at various times I also joined a choir group, dance performances, fashion shows, a local advocacy group, and other groups that benefit the community.

Although I was constantly reminded by my friends and colleagues that I overburdened myself with so many activities and responsibilities, I dismissed their concerns. Instead, I prayed solemnly to God to give me direction. I clamored for

God's purpose in me so much that I began to slowly drop most of my secular activities. I then started refocusing the direction of my thoughts toward God's kingdom priority. Clearly, God answered my prayers. I slowly began to notice changes in my lifestyle. I daily prayed to God, "In your dwelling place, my God and my Savior, I surrender my life to you for your kingdom impact."

The most profound impact on me was my husband's transformed life perspective and his relationship with God. I gradually felt his faith and love for the Lord. This was further attested by his regular church attendance and his reading of God's Word. Our daily devotions and prayers to our heavenly Father helped us grow together in spiritual maturity in our relationship with God. In so doing, it allowed us both to redefine the true meaning of our relationship with God, family, and others. It also reignited our true love and compassion for each other and, most importantly, it rebuilt my trust in him. Our relationship with God became stronger as we united in prayer, in faith, and in love instead of my seeking solace in God by myself. I began to understand God's purpose for us, as stated in Colossians 2:2: "My purpose is that they may be encouraged in heart and united in love, so that they may have the full riches of complete understanding, in order that they may know the mystery of God, namely, Christ."

Our obedience and faithfulness to the Lord granted us access to God's blessings. We prayed to God as exhorted in Philippians 4:6, "Do not be anxious about anything, but in everything, by prayer and petition, with thanksgiving, present your requests to God."

In God's time, our prayers are answered. I am most certain that this book is the answer to my prayers. I thank God for answered prayer. It is therefore my conviction that God is using me through my career as a financial advisor with a Christian perspective, as I claim my practice as His purpose for me.

***The third step is fellowship***. In 1 Corinthians 12:12, it is said, "The body is a unit, though it is made up of many parts; and though all its parts are many, they form one body. So it is with Christ." That being said, we are parts of one body in Jesus Christ. Romans 12:5 also says, "So in Christ we who are many form one body, and each member belongs to all the others." Each part of the body is uniquely created; thus our uniqueness makes us complement each other through our fellowship with God and with others. Again, this is attested in 1 Corinthians 12:14: "Now the body is not made up of one part but of many." This is likewise attested in Romans 12:4: "Just as each of us has one body with many members, and these members do not all have the same function."

God's purpose for each of us will be made known to us if we seek Him with all our mind, body, and soul. Our relationship with God and others is crucial to realizing that purpose. God is light, and if we walk in the light we have fellowship with Him. This is what 1 John 1:7 says: "But if we walk in the light, as He is in the light, we have fellowship with one another, and the blood of Jesus, his Son, purifies us from all sin.

I make myself available to God in fellowship through my teaching of a Bible study group and also as I claim my practice as financial advisor as being for His purpose.

***The last step is discipleship.*** Jesus invites us to be His disciples. Accepting His loving invitation comes with commitment and sacrifice. In Luke 14:33, Jesus said, "In the same way, any of you who does not give up everything he has cannot be my disciple." At my church, I attended a class on discipleship conducted by Martin and Beth Sanders. During the study, Beth showed us how to witness to others. At that very instant I felt God's intervention, and I was convicted to start witnessing to others. My heart agonized for my family, especially for my mother, whom I knew believed in the Lord but had never received Him as her Savior and Lord. That very same day, I asked four people at the class to pray for me and for my heart's desire to witness to others, especially my mother. Two days later, I was able to share with my mother God's love and plan for her. Since then I have become committed to continually witness to others at every opportunity I have. I also pray that through this book people will come to God and build a personal relationship with Him.

Relationship with God is yielding control of your life to God, thus allowing Him to intervene in your daily life. We must strive to be fully dependent upon God, because God's love for us is unconditional. If we commit sins, He is just to forgive us. This is critical to a loving relationship between God and man and thus critical to our journey heavenward.

***Heavenly Father:***

*As I continue to build my personal relationship with You,*
*I must completely surrender my life to You.*
*Deciding where to go, what to do, and with whom to do it*
*Should be a reflection of my total allegiance to You.*

*Thank you, Father:*

*For revealing your purpose to me*
*To be rightly related to You*
*As I make a difference in the lives of many.*

*Thank you, Father:*

*For giving me the wisdom to write this book*
*To send a message of hope and encouragement*

*Above all, thank You, Father:*

*For what you have done in my life*
*And in the life of my husband,*
*For together we now can share*
*The true meaning of our relationships*
*To you, Father,*

*To our family,*
*And to others.*
*AMEN.*

***Personal Reflection (Personal Relationship with God)*:**

- How is your personal relationship with God?
- How are you honoring God with His provisions?
- Describe some of your answered prayers.
- Do you allow God to intervene in your daily life? How?
- Describe how the four-step process has enhanced your daily walk with God.
- Write your personal prayer.

## *Family Relationship: Spouse*

In Ephesians 5:22-24, we read, "Wives, submit to your husbands as to the Lord. For the husband is the head of the wife as Christ is the head of the church, his body, of which he is the Savior. Now as the church submits to Christ, so also wives should submit to their husbands in everything." Sometimes this passage is misinterpreted or misread to say that a man has the right to subject his wife. This is not the case. Instead, the wife in a godly, selfless way is to submit to her husband's authority. According to The Bible and the Wife's Responsibility to the Husband (www.bible.ca), the wife and husband are to be partners, working together toward a common goal. The wife must be appreciative of her husband's actions, efforts, and work in supporting the family. It is therefore the wife's responsibility to make sure that her husband feels comfortable and happy when he comes home.

During the early years of my marriage, I felt for my husband's lack of confidence in his decision making, especially when it came to finances. I then took the role of making all the major financial decisions. Since my background was in finance, it came very easily for me to handle money. This arrangement worked well, for the most part, in my married life. But after I discovered God's Word, I began to have a better understanding that marriage leadership has to be shared in mutual respect. Leadership between spouses is a function that should always be shared as they share love, work, and opportunities. Although I didn't feel any competition or conflicts in my decision-making process, I have to admit that, on a few occasions, there were struggles for control. Now I realize that this could have contributed to some of the problems in my marriage relationship. It is therefore my conviction to work things out and to change my perspective in life in accordance with God's law. There are many practices and decisions I wish I had handled differently. Had I known then what I know now, maybe things could have been better. Like the psalmist in Psalm 16:2, I now say to the Lord, "You are my Lord; apart from you I have no good thing." God is the only source of all things that are pure and true. My personal message to wives is to take this opportunity to reflect and examine your relationship with your spouse. Pray for God's guidance about what to do. Ephesians 5:25-28 declares,

> Husbands, love your wives, just as Christ loved the church and gave himself up for her, to make her holy, cleansing her by the washing with water through the word, and to present her to himself as a radiant church, without stain or wrinkle or any other blemish, but holy and blameless. In this same way, husbands ought to love their wives as their own bodies. He who loves his wife loves himself.

God loves us, and that love was demonstrated by His sacrificial act of sending His Son to die for our sins. Therefore a husband's love for his wife requires a sacrifice. This sacrifice must be carried out in kindness motivated by a desire to make his wife happy. It must be the husband's goal to build her up in order to bring about God's purpose in her. It is stated in Colossians 3:19, "Husbands, love your wives and do not be harsh with them." Husbands must be sensitive to the needs of their wives, know what they are good at, know their talents, and help them develop those talents. In most cases this is not the reality, but it is the dream of most women to have a husband like this. It was my dream.

There were lots of challenges during the early years of my marriage, and my relationship with my husband was a constant struggle. I must say that not having God as our stronghold in my early marriage derailed us from the path to a godly relationship. Many years ago, a very dear friend of mine shared with me about her husband's ongoing unfaithfulness to her. Out of curiosity, I began to question how they managed to stay together after all these years of his being unfaithful to her. Much to my amazement, she said to me hang on to your man; divorce is not a solution. Indeed, more than thirty-five years later, they are still married. Another friend of mine with almost the same situation ended up getting divorced. But there's more to the story. They got back together after a few years. Today they are living a normal relationship. I began to wonder if this is how God brought humor to life.

During the course of my practice as a financial advisor, I came across many couples who had a lot of challenges in their marital relationship. They shared their stories as I shared mine, and to my surprise, there were unimaginable situations that were deemed unforgivable. But God is awesome because He gives us ample room to forgive. At first, I was not comfortable dealing with these issues, but over time I became more competent and comfortable. With my faith in the Lord, I became more compassionate toward everybody. Not only did I become their financial advisor, but I also became their life planner. I became prayerful. I began to ask the Spirit of God to speak to me to illuminate me and open my heart and my life for other people, as I meditated on Ephesians 1:17-18:

> I keep asking that the God of our Lord Jesus Christ, the glorious Father, may give you the Spirit of wisdom and revelation, so that you may know him better. I pray also that the eyes of your heart may be enlightened in order that you may know the hope to which he has called you, the riches of his glorious inheritance in the saints.

Genesis 2:24 describes what happens when a man and a woman get married: "For this reason a man will leave his father and mother and be united to his wife, and they will become one flesh." Then in 1 Corinthians 7:4, it is said further that "the wife's body does not belong to her alone but also to her husband. In the same way, the husband's body does not belong to him alone but also to his wife." Therefore, it is very important for husband and wife to be obedient, trustworthy, and respectful of each other. Unfortunately, there often are lots of betrayed trusts that bring turmoil into a relationship. But God is just to forgive us of our iniquities. Husbands and wives, present your petitions to the Lord, pray without ceasing, trust in Him, seek Him, and He will guide your path.

***Heavenly Father:***

*In You I trust; teach me Your paths.*
*In Your truth, guide me in Your ways,*
*for You are my Savior and Lord,*
*and my hope is in You all day long.*

*Father, I solemnly say this prayer for me and my husband:*
*Whatever our differences,*
*Lord, lift our spirit.*
*Whatever our trials,*
*Lord, lift our soul.*

*Whatever our worries,*
*Lord, lift our mind.*
*Whatever our pains,*
*Lord, lift our bodies.*
*Forgive our iniquities,*
*Lord, our Savior. AMEN.*

***Prayer of a Wife:***

*I will give thanks unto the Lord:*
*for my husband and my marriage,*
*for his love and his protection.*
*I will give thanks unto the Lord:*
*that I have someone to encourage and to love,*
*that I have someone beside me wherever I go,*
*that I have someone behind me, supporting me in whatever I do.*
*I don't have to face the world alone.*
*I don't have to face my family alone.*
*But only in You, God, must I appear before the judgment seat of Christ*
*that I may receive the gift of eternal life. AMEN.*

***Personal Reflection (Family Relationship: Spouse):***

- What specific changes must you make in order to love your spouse the way Christ loves His church?
- State your major concern or challenges affecting your marriage relationship.
- What will you have to give up to accommodate each other as partners?
- Describe your feelings for your spouse right now.
- Write your personal prayer.

## *Family Relationship: Children*

There's nothing more challenging than raising children and guiding them to be accountable to God. When our children were babies, we lovingly cared for them, fed them, and rocked them to sleep. Likewise, our heavenly Father is involved in our spiritual growth. Through His Word, He encourages and cares for us. No matter how challenging it is to raise our children, we must teach them well, and our words and actions should be in accordance with the teaching of the Lord. In Ephesians 6:1-3, it is said, "Children, obey your parents in the Lord, for this is right. Honor your father and mother which is the first commandment with a promise so that it may go well with you and that you may enjoy long life on the earth."

Being a mother to two daughters (Trisha, now 28, and Karina, now 26) did not come very easily. Like every mother, my wish was to give my daughters the best in life. In my culture, I was brought up with the idea that education is the top priority in life. I, likewise, instilled this very same concept in my children's minds as they were growing. Both excelled in school and were identified as gifted students. Before they entered kindergarten, I made sure that they were both taught how to read and write. Karina was academically advanced for her age and started reading at age four.

Neither Trisha nor Karina was into the typical girl activities; instead, they were into sports. Mostly they played soccer, and they both were on highly competitive traveling teams. Often their teams competed in different major cities and states. The eight years they were playing soccer were the most significant and enjoyable years we had together as a family. The competition was almost year-round, and every weekend we traveled together, as a family, for their games.

Trisha and Karina were also active members of the Girls Scouts of America. At high school, Karina became actively involved in the school marching band and jazz band, playing trumpet and trombone. There was no idle time for my children during their teenage years. I also made sure that I got involved in some of their school activities by volunteering. Between schools, sports, libraries, and many other extracurricular activities for my daughters, there were many responsibilities, but I enjoyed every moment of them. Academically, Trisha and Karina did very well, from elementary to high school.

I have to admit, though, that God was not the center of our lives then, although part of our Sunday's schedule was to attend church. It was a whole lot different without God as the stronghold in our relationships.

Trisha was turning sixteen and Karina was fourteen when they were introduced to the Lord as their Savior. We then started to attend a small church called the New Beginning Community Church. Trisha became an active member of the worship team, and Karina got involved in the music, where she played the trumpet. It was also during those years that my marriage was in jeopardy. I did not know how much damage the pain I was suffering from the shaky marriage brought to my daughters. All that I knew was I became stricter and meaner to them. Subconsciously, maybe I was taking out my anger and frustration on them. I guess I did not know how to handle my emotions very well. When my anger and frustration hit me, I had the tendency to overreact very easily.

As I continued to seek the Lord, my anger and frustration began to mellow. Many times I prayed so hard my favorite Scriptures, Psalm 20:1 and 4: "May the Lord answer you when you are in distress; may the name of the God of Jacob protect you. . . . May He give you the desire of your heart and make all your plans succeed."

If I am to put together parenting guidelines, I must first focus on the parents' marriage relationship. Consider evaluating any preexisting marital problems, and, most importantly, pray to God. Then seek Christian professional counseling, if needed. Even though parents desire their children's safety and well-being, a bad marriage relationship could damage the children's future. I must admit that every time I got mad at my children, I ended up crying all night long and wished it had never happened. I always became apologetic to them. Karina used to say to me that I was very lucky that both she and her sister grew up to be responsible children. All I could say then was, "Indeed, I was so blessed for having you as my daughters." Now I can honestly say that I resented every moment that I allowed myself to become angry and bitter. I asked God to forgive me for what I had done wrong and also asked my children's forgiveness. In retrospect, this is what I tell my children again and again, "God knew what the desire of my heart was for you, and He did not allow you to become rebellious and irresponsible children, and I love you very much."

Trisha finished college and earned her degree in biology at age twenty-one at the University of San Diego. Karina did exceptionally well in college and earned a degree in psychology. She graduated as an honor student from the University of California at Los Angeles when she was just twenty years old. I thank God for blessing me with two wonderful daughters. I will ever be grateful and thankful to God for them. Maybe some parents were not as fortunate with their children, but I would like to share one very important thing with these parents: pray for your children and love them even more. I would like to share God's promises in Proverbs 22:6: "Train a child in the way he should go, and when he is old he will not turn from it." Also Proverbs 13:24 says, "He who spares the rod hates his son, but he who loves him is careful to discipline him." I always wished I had known the Lord early on in my life so that I had been guided and directed by His Word in my parenting skills. But, nonetheless, it is not too late for the Lord. Even now that our daughters are grown up, every day my husband and I are constantly praying for them. My daily prayer for my children is that God may provide them the spirit of wisdom and revelation to know Him more as they walk with Him in truth and in love. Sometimes I worry over their relationship with the Lord, but again I know that there is always hope for the future. After all, my timing is not God's timing.

Ephesians 6:4 says, "Fathers, do not exasperate your children; instead, bring them up in the training and instruction of the Lord." According to The Bible and the Wife's Responsibility to the Husband (www.bible.ca), children can become exasperating at times, but remember, they are children who are still developing and learning. They need that guiding hand of their parents that lets them know that they are the objects of their love and concern. Indeed, it is God's command to love our children.

***Heavenly Father**:*

*Thank You for blessing me and my husband with two lovely daughters and an admirable son-in-law.*

*Thank you to my daughter **Trisha** as I say:

T -Truly you're lovely
R -Responsible in every way
I -Integrity is your priority
S -Sincere in feelings
H-Humble in actions
A-Amazing, that's how you are to mommy! AMEN.

*Thank you to my daughter **Karina** as I say:

K-Kindness is in your heart
A-Almighty God you love
R-Respect and honor
I- Instructed in your life
N-Numerous successes by your side
A-Always and forever you light up my life! AMEN.

*Thank you to my son-in-law **Daniel** as I say:

D-Dedicated husband you are to Trisha
A-Admirable son-in-law you are to Rey and Tess
N-Never-ending fun you are to Karina
I -Inspirational you are to Joshua
E-Everlasting guidance you are to Melissa
L-Loving son you are to Bruce and Sue. AMEN.

***Personal Reflection (Family Relationship: Children):***

- If you have children, what are the challenges in your parenting experiences?
- Be thankful to God for your children.
- Do you have any testimonies of God's grace in the raising of your children?
- Write your prayer.

## *Relationships with Others*

There are various ways we are accountable to God and to others in our everyday lives. Hebrews 13:16 says, "And do not forget to do good and to share with others, for with such sacrifices God is pleased." One of the qualities of a good person is kindness toward others. This is supported in 1 Timothy 6:18: "Command them to do good, to be rich in good deeds, and to be generous and willing to share."

We must love others compassionately. However, there are some things we must understand and examine in ourselves before we can honestly say that we love others compassionately. In Luke 10:27, Jesus said, "Love the Lord your God with all your heart and with all your soul and with all your strength and with all your mind; and love your neighbor as yourself." First and foremost, we must love God completely with all our soul, strength, and mind. To completely love God is to submit our lives to Him. Second, we must love ourselves honestly and truthfully. According to Ken Boa, being honest and truthful with ourselves, we are free to love and serve others without seeking our own interests first. Because of our strong faith in God, we feel confident in ourselves that we don't have to prove anything to others. We do not allow ourselves to be controlled by the opinions and responses of others. Needless to say, we can do our work with dignity and excellence without trying to impress and manipulate people. Our focus should be our relationship with God and what He thinks of us rather than what others think of us.

My business is helping people in their financial planning regarding retirement, and many people ask me when I plan to retire. Usually I tell them, I don't plan to retire because I love what I do and I intend to work as long as God allows me to. I am passionate about the things I do because it is giving me purpose and meaning. To serve others is God's greatest gift to mankind. Every day that I talk to people is an opportunity to help, but I also look at it as a great opportunity to grow. You would be surprised how much wisdom and knowledge people can give you. Networking, to me, is not just a good source of business referrals but also a great opportunity to share God's love and purpose. Indeed, there are both wealth and information found in helping others.

God has, through our faith, assured us of eternal life in His kingdom, but before then, we must be in accord with God's will for us. Here on earth we are passersby; all the things we do and all the things we have are temporary. Yet too often we treat life as if it will be permanent. This seems to be a dilemma that has brought us into a lot of confusion and misguidance in life. We always want to position ourselves to be the best, but the best is not good enough after a while. We constantly long for power, fame, material possessions, and much more. There will never be an end to what we want in life. After I have said all of this, I just want to kneel down before Jesus and boldly say, "Jesus, I am sorry for all the wrong things I've done. Please forgive me. Thank You for opening my eyes, ears, and heart for Your kingdom purpose. And thank You, Jesus, for the change in my heart for Your honor and glory. Amen."

## *Love One Another*

***Heavenly Father:***

**L**- Loving one another is a virtue that edifies
**O**-Obedient to God exceedingly gratifies
**V**- Victory now proclaimed to God's glory
**E**- Excellent is your name, God Almighty

**O**-Only in God and others do we find true fellowship
**N**-Nonetheless compassionate and real friendship
**E**- Entrusted with secrets too sacred in a relationship

**A**-Another time, day, and year could have gone by
**N**-Newer and better experience shall always pass by
**O**-Only through God we must greatly devour
**T**- To worship and to pray, until the end of the hour
**H**- Hope, love, and peace more virtues to keep
**E**- Everlasting friendship every one must be equipped
**R**- Relationship with God, family, and others heavenward we commit. *AMEN.*

***Personal Reflection (Relationships with Others):***

- How are your relationships with others?
- Do you have any testimonies of God's work in your relationships?
- Write your personal prayer.

***

## *Chapter Three*

# GOD-DRIVEN PURPOSE

### *Worship*

In Luke 4:8, Jesus told Satan, "It is written: 'Worship the Lord your God and serve him only.'" When we worship the Lord our God, we are showing reverence and gratitude to Him. Christians worship the Lord in many different ways. Nehemiah 8:6 says, "Ezra praised the Lord, the great God; and all the people lifted their hands and responded, 'Amen! Amen!' Then they bowed down and worshiped the Lord with their faces to the ground." The music portion of the church service could be another way of worshiping the Lord. Whether in church, at home, or anywhere, we can be worshiping the Lord.

According to Billy Graham, in Christian worship there is the inner longing for God to come into our lives such that we want to verbalize, vocalize, and put into action those feelings. We want to communicate that there is one God worthy of our worship. Through worship we acknowledge that we love God and we are thankful for what He has done for us through His Son Jesus Christ. It was said that God created us to glorify Him, and worshiping Him is clearly of interest to and a delight to God. Whatever our position in life, whether we are a preacher, a doctor, an engineer, a salesperson, a waiter, or a janitor, we can do everything for the glory of God. It is my fervent hope and prayer that the lives we live be an act of worship to Him.

In my heart, it is my conviction that my practice as a financial advisor with a Christian perspective is God's purpose for me. I look at everything that has happened in my life as part of the process of making me who I am. I prayed to God and asked for strength, but He gave me problems; so I asked for wisdom, and He gave me much learning to live by. My earliest recollection as a young girl was living in a laid-back countryside (or *barrio*) without electricity. I had to walk miles to get to a nearby town. I remember that the only time we could play outside the house at night was when there was moonlight. All the children in the *barrio* were gathered to play by the street or at the courtyard. Most of the time our parents also gathered to tell us stories. My favorite was my grandfather's storytelling time. He loved to tell stories about the Bible, although he never told us the source. But all the time I saw him reading a black book. It was only when I started reading the Bible that I came to realize that my grandfather's stories were from the Bible. He was full of wisdom, and at a young age, I was always amazed at his stories and how visionary my grandfather was. As I come to think of it right now, his way of telling things and doing things was his way of *worshiping the Lord*. As a young girl, I must have picked up some of this wisdom, for it helped mold me into the person I am today. I used to listen to his stories a lot, and then I began to apply them in my life. I grew up hardworking, creative, and responsible. I learned to earn my allowance at an early age. I developed a habit of believing that if I was told to do things I might as well do it with the right attitude. My grandfather loved the Lord, and although he didn't say it very often, I must have felt it from his love for me.

In Philippians 2:9-11, it is written, "Therefore God exalted him to the highest place and gave him the name that is above every name, that at the name of Jesus every knee should bow, in heaven and on earth and under the earth, and every tongue confess that Jesus Christ is Lord, to the glory of God the Father." He alone is worthy of our worship and praise. Therefore, if you believe Jesus is Lord, why do you have to wait? All you have to do is believe in your heart that Jesus died for your sins and rose again. Pray and ask Him to come into your life and be your Savior and Lord. Exodus 23:25 says, "Worship the Lord your God and his blessing will be on your food and water. I will take away sickness from among you."

***Heavenly Father:***

*We worship You with reverence and gratitude.*
*We honor You with thanksgiving prayers.*
*We glorify You with delightful hearts.*
*We worship You, honor You, and glorify You.*
*Our Father in Heaven, hallowed is Thy name. AMEN.*

***Personal Reflection (Worship):***

- Do you let the life you live be an act of worship to God?
- What impact you have on others is a way of worshiping the Lord?
- Do you have a testimony relating to your worship of the Lord?
- Write your personal prayer.

## *Fellowship*

In the mainstream of secular life, fellowship is not a word that is used much. The *American Heritage Dictionary* defines fellowship as, "The condition of sharing similar interests, ideals, or experiences, as by reason of profession, religion, or nationality." Fellowship is simply a group of people getting together in the same place for the same purpose. There is usually a strong bond of friendship. It is said in 1 John 1:7, "But if we walk in the light, as he is in the light, we have fellowship with one another, and the blood of Jesus, his Son, purifies us from all sin." In Christian fellowship we believe that we are one body in Christ, and thus each of us can form close relationships in support of our spiritual growth. Together in Christ, we are brothers and sisters.

In 1 John 1:3, it is also said, "We proclaim to you what we have seen and heard, so that you also may have fellowship with us. And our fellowship is with the Father and with his Son, Jesus Christ." Fellowship is necessary for Christians to help others live godly lives through the study of God's Word. Through fellowship, Christians provide comfort and compassion when someone is grieving over a loss of loved ones, lend emotional support to a friend who is going through a tough time at work or at home, and offer helping hands to fellow believers to find the inner strength to follow God's leading in their lives.

At my church there are several ministries available for each member to access and join. Basically these are ways where we fellowship with one another. Proverbs 27:17 says, "As iron sharpens iron, so one man sharpens another." This analogy is telling us that we need one another. Fellowship is a way to reach out to fellow Christians who can nurture us and mentor us about our relationship with God and others. There are lots of Bible study groups that anybody can join. This may serve as a support team to help each member grow in his or her walk with God. Christian fellowship is one of our God-driven purposes. Could it be that this is your purpose?

***Heavenly Father:***

*I thank You that I was given the opportunity to serve You through my Bible study group, thus, enabling all of us to learn your Word and fellowship with You and others. Thank You, Father, for what You have done in their lives and in their relationships with one another. We give You the honor, praise, and glory. In Jesus' wonderful name. AMEN.*

***Personal Reflection (Fellowship)***:

- What does Christian fellowship mean to you?
- What benefits does Christian fellowship provide you?

- Do you have any testimony regarding Christian fellowship?
- Write your personal prayer.

## *Ministry*

I am a member of an organization called Kingdom Advisors. Ron Blue, the president of Kingdom Advisors, in his letter to KA members, stated that Kingdom Advisors exists as a ministry to support Christian financial professionals like myself to unleash kingdom influence in our practice and in our clients. Its vision is for every Christian financial professional to make his or her practice their ministry and to release life-changing principles of Biblical wisdom resulting in kingdom impact. Kingdom Advisors now ministers and serves more than three thousand Christian financial professionals. The organization is witnessing incredible life change as advisors find purpose and meaning in their work like never before and as clients experience true joy and financial freedom through kingdom impact. (The website for Kingdom Advisors is www.KINGDOM ADVISORS.ORG)

> Recent economic volatility reinforced Kingdom Advisors' belief that timeless Biblical financial principles are being embraced by a public looking for answers. We have witnessed a flourishing movement of Christian financial professionals responding to God's call to serve clients by integrating their faith and their work . . . professionals who are hungry for guidance, direction, and resources to fulfill that mission.

These statements were taken from the *Kingdom Advisors Lifeline, Quarterly Ministry Update* 2009. It was further stated that being a member of Kingdom Advisors provides us purpose and meaning in our work as we minister to clients by guiding conversations that encourage clients to reflect on their life purpose, joy, and generosity. Accordingly, Kingdom Advisors is supporting a real movement that is gaining intensity around the country. Furthermore, the movement is confident that the ministry model was God's calling for Kingdom Advisors, because together with the members, they are changing financial paradigms in America for lasting impact.

Being a member of Kingdom Advisors, coupled with my love for the Lord, has allowed me to transform the concept of my financial planning practice. Integrating Scriptures into my practice provided me wisdom to share timeless Biblical financial principles to my clients. The Kingdom Advisors speaker series truly enhances my growth, introspection, and life change for integrating my faith into my practice. This process of building my kingdom business is being refined and advanced during the interactive and truly informative sessions with Ron Blue and other dynamic speakers during the coaching calls. It further inspired me to be more passionate with my practice, giving me more opportunities and greater desire to share God's love by witnessing to people.

Acknowledging that God put me here on earth temporarily and for a purpose, it is important for me to do what God called me to do and to do it now. I have no second chance to prepare for my eternal consequences as each day is an opportunity and privilege. It is my hope and prayer that when I come face to face with the Lord, I can hear Jesus say, "Well done, good and faithful servant! You have been faithful with a few things; I will put you in charge of many things. Come and share your master's happiness!" (Matthew 25.21). What about you?

***Heavenly Father:***

*I thank You for the Kingdom Advisors organization, its mission and vision. I thank You that integrating Scripture into my practice provided me wisdom to share timeless Biblical financial principles with my clients.*

*I thank You for Ron Blue, Rob West, Randy Glass, and other dynamic speakers who truly enhanced my growth and life change. I thank You that integrating my faith into my practice truly is an answer to God's call. AMEN.*

***Personal Reflection (Ministry):***

- What is your ministry?
- Is there any ministry that has impacted your life and your relationship with God?
- What is your conviction, if any, with regard to ministry?
- Write your personal prayer.

## *Discipleship*

There is a cost to being a disciple. As Jesus said in Luke 14:33, "In the same way, any of you who does not give up everything he has cannot be my disciple." As true disciples, Pastor Martin and Beth Sanders illustrate this Scripture. Eight years ago, God sent them to do a discipleship ministry in Asia, centered in the Philippines. Pastor Martin and Beth, together with their three children had to leave behind the luxury of an American lifestyle that many people aspire to have in order to accomplish God's mission. They practically gave up everything they had to do what God called them to do. With God's provision, they were blessed far beyond their expectation with a ministry to great numbers. Being faithful and obedient to God paved their way to a better and greater reward for their children's education, and those children are now in college, pursuing godly lives of their own.

As they continue what they started, God calls them, from time to time, to different areas of the world to serve. Their reaching out to people through their ministry in Asia did not limit their territorial boundaries. Whenever and wherever they get the opportunity, they faithfully share God's message.

I met Pastor Martin and Beth when they came back to San Diego for furlough. I belong to the same church they were serving before they went to the mission field. While in San Diego, through the Maranatha Women's Ministry, Beth taught and shared the discipleship concept of reaching out to people. Her inspiring love and faithfulness to God were clearly revealed. Through this class, I was able to learn how to witness to people. From that day forward, I have been witnessing to family, friends, and clients.

Pastor Martin and Beth Sanders brought significant kingdom impact to my life, and especially to my husband Rey. God brought this couple into our lives and used them mightily to enlighten much confusion in my husband's relationship with the Lord. Although he received the Lord many years ago, it did not seem to matter much compared to the day of his spiritual rebirth when Pastor Martin shared with him about rebuilding his relationship with God. I thank God for His grace, mercy, and love as it is attested in Lamentations 3:22-23, "Because of the Lord's great love we are not consumed, for his compassions never fail. They are new every morning; great is your faithfulness." Indeed, it was quite a transformation in the life of my husband and his relationship with God. Since then, my husband and I have been reaching out to God through our daily devotions and prayers, which certainly defines the true meaning of life in our relationship to God and to each other. I can never thank God enough for using Pastor Martin and Beth to make a difference in our lives.

Part of Pastor Martin and Beth's holistic mission statement is the Great Commission found in Matthew 28:19-20: "Therefore go and make disciples of all nations, baptizing them in the name of the Father and of the Son and of the Holy Spirit, and teaching them to obey everything I have commanded you. And surely I am with you always, to the very end of the age."

***Heavenly Father:***

*Thank You for Pastor Martin and Beth Sanders,*
*For their obedience to Your godly calling,*
*For their faithfulness to make disciples of people,*
*And for their kingdom impact in our lives and the lives of many others. AMEN.*

***Personal Reflection (Discipleship):***

- What is your conviction about discipleship?
- Do you have a personal testimony regarding discipleship?
- Write your personal prayer.

***

## *Chapter Four*

# LIFESTYLE (Way of Life): IS GOD IN CONTROL?

### *Spiritual—Faith*

Man wants to be needed. Feelings of acceptance, affection, and companionship are necessary for our personal fulfillment. It is always the case that we don't get all that we want and the emotional satisfaction we crave. Sometimes we feel so empty that we resort to doing things in a desperate search for personal fulfillment. Without satisfaction, we spend time, money, and other resources just to fill the void. More often than not, we end up more dissatisfied than ever. What we don't realize is that spiritual intimacy is so fulfilling that we become less dependent upon human relationships and material possessions. This is a true test of our faith in God. In Ephesians 3:17, Paul prayed, "that Christ may dwell in your heart through faith."

I can easily relate to this situation by what happened to a dear friend of mine. I will call her Ms. G. For most of Ms. G's married life, her husband worked a thousand miles away from home. Over that period of time, when they were far apart from each other, the husband had an extramarital affair with another woman; then there were kids from that affair. My friend was surely devastated, but she could not do anything. She endured years of pain and suffering. Somehow she managed to take care for her life, but she felt lonely, angry, and confused. She tried to look for relief and resorted to gambling. She admitted to me that by going to the casinos she finds relief, almost like an escape from all her worries. It was not easy for me to see her suffer and to try to deal with her gambling issues. Her emotional and financial dilemma was overwhelming. I prayed to God about how I could help her. I reached out to her, told her that God loves her, and witnessed to her. I praise God for this opportunity. She's still trying to work things out with her relationship with the Lord and hopefully to let go of some of her problems. She needs faith and hope, for, as Hebrews 11:1 says, "Now faith is being sure of what we hope for and certain of what we do not see."

Another friend with a similar gambling problem claimed that his frustration with family relationships was the cause of it. He and his wife seemed to disagree about a lot of financial decision making. He also claimed that his resentment contributed to the craving for physical attention and emotional satisfaction. As I said earlier, man wants to be needed, and the feeling of acceptance, affection, and companionship are necessary to our personal fulfillment. Often we tend to exacerbate the real problem by resorting to what we think is quicker and faster relief and end up creating even more critical problems. Relatively speaking, my husband's affair with another woman could have been caused, in part, by his longing for my full attention to his needs, for when our daughters were little, I certainly agree that most of my attention was focused on them. These are some of the danger signs in a relationship that we need to pay closer attention to.

As I also said earlier, what we don't really realize is that spiritual intimacy is so fulfilling that we become less dependent upon human relationships and material possessions. It is therefore my conviction that we need to turn over to God all our worries in order to get relief from all these challenging situations. I can't overemphasize how we need God to intervene in this process and in our lives. Indeed, I thank God that I was able to reach out to these families and share with them God's love and the gift of salvation. We must cling to our faith in God.

***Heavenly Father:***

*In You, Lord, there is faith*
*That we learn to accept our shortcomings.*
*In You, Lord, there is hope*
*That we learn to deal with our challenges,*
*For without You, Lord,*
*There is no faith; there is no hope.*
*Then surely we are nothing. AMEN.*

***Personal Reflection (Spiritual—Faith):***

- Describe your spiritual walk with God.
- What are your challenges?
- Describe your faith versus your fear.
- Write your personal prayer.

## *Financial—Wealth (Financial Stewardship)*

Set your minds on things above, not on earthly things. (Colossians 3:2)

Did you know that there are more than 2,300 verses in the Bible that relate to money and possessions? Considering our present financial crisis today, with job layoffs, inflation, declining stock market, consumer debts, no cash reserves, no retirement, no college funds, mortgage defaults, and decline in home values, it is likely you are asking some of these questions: How is all this affecting us personally? How can we thrive during economic uncertainty? What is our priority, and is it worldly or godly? Is God's Word relevant to how we use our talent, work, time, and resources? And how can being faithful to God help us become better managers? I strongly believe that all of the above questions can be answered by posing another question: Who owns it all?

In this segment of my book, I would like to share a concept I developed called Bible-driven financial strategies. These are Biblical principles, or wisdom, that will guide us on how to manage our finances. First, we have to understand what the Bible has to say about the importance of financial plans. Proverbs 16:9 says, "In his heart a man plans his course, but the Lord determines his steps." Proverbs 16:3 says, "Commit to the Lord whatever you do and your plans will succeed." And in Proverbs 13:11, it is said, "Dishonest money dwindles away, but he who gathers money little by little makes it grow." We are being reminded by these Scriptures that, as we make our financial plans, we need to be guided by God's commands on how to handle our material blessings, and we need to be good stewards of our time, talent, abilities, and financial resources.

The following topics are the focus of our study.

- Biblical principles of managing our financial resources
- Objectives of financial planning
- Process of sctting up a financial plan
- Biblical principles for a successful financial plan

The following are Biblical principles of managing our financial resources:

1. Recognizing God's ownership
2. Realizing that we are God's stewards/managers
3. Understanding God's on guard against all kinds of greed
4. Acknowledging that we are accountable to God
5. Being faithful and obedient to God's will in our lives

*1. Recognizing God's ownership.* God owns everything. He is the Master of all. We are His creation, and He knows what's going on in us. The following are Scriptures that relate to God's ownership: Psalm 24:1: "The earth is the Lord's, and everything in it, the world, and all who live in it"; 1 Chronicles

29:12: "Wealth and honor come from you; you are the ruler of all things. In your hands are strength and power to exalt and give strength to all."

2. *Realizing that we are God's stewards/managers.* According to Ron Blue, Biblical stewardship is the use of God-given resources for the accomplishment of God-given goals and objectives. In Luke 16:11-13, Jesus said,

> So if you have not been trustworthy in handling worldly wealth, who will trust you with true riches. And if you have not been trustworthy with someone else's property, who will give you property of your own. No servant can serve two masters; either he will hate the one and love the other or he will be devoted to the one and despise the other. You can not serve both God and money.

First Corinthians 4:2 says, "Now it is required that those who have been given a trust must prove faithful." Also 1 Peter 4:10 says, "Each one should use whatever gift he has received to serve others, faithfully administering God's grace in its various forms."

3. *Understanding God's on guard against all kinds of greed.* First Timothy 6:9-10 warns us about the love of money: "People who want to get rich fall into temptation and a trap and into many foolish and harmful desires that plunge men into ruin and destruction. For the love of money is a root of all kinds of evil. Some people, eager for money, have wandered from the faith and pierced themselves with many griefs." In Luke 12:15, we are warned about being greedy: "Then he said to them, 'Watch out! Be on guard against all kinds of greed, a man's life does not consist in the abundance of his possessions.'" In Hebrews 13:5 is an awesome promise of God to us, and it is connected to a command to do the right thing: "Keep your lives free from the love of money and be content with what you have, because God has said, never will I leave you, never will I forsake you." Not

only is the love of money a source of all kinds of evil, but Ecclesiastes 5:10 also tells us how we are never satisfied with material things: "Whoever loves money never has money enough, whoever loves wealth is never satisfied with his income."

4. *Acknowledging that we are accountable to God.* Our accountability is to God for all the things we have done on earth. First and foremost, as Exodus 20:3 says, "You shall have no other gods before me." From God's supremacy, it follows that "each of us will give an account of himself to God" (Romans 14:12). The consequences of not acknowledging our accountability to God is described in Ecclesiastes 12:13-14: "Fear God and keep his commandments, for this is the whole duty of man, for God will bring every deed into judgment, including every hidden thing, whether it is good or evil." Hebrews 4:13 confirms our accountability: "Nothing in all creation is hidden from God's sight. Everything is uncovered and laid bare before the eyes of him to whom we must give account."

5. *Being faithful and obedient to God's will in our lives.* Psalm 32:8 says, "I will instruct you and teach you in the way you should go, I will counsel you and watch over you." And Psalm 37:23-24 says, "If the Lord delights in a man's way, He makes his steps firm; Though he stumble, he will not fall, for the Lord upholds him with his hands." Our God's faithfulness to His promises is attested by all these Scriptures. And Philippians 2:13 explains, "For it is God who works in you to will and to act according to his good purpose."

In setting up your financial goals, there are both short-term and long-term objectives. Short-term financial objectives can be established through a personalized series of questions to determine how you are dealing with your present financial situations. (A) *Are you giving back to God*? Proverbs 3:9 says, "Honor the Lord with your wealth, with the first fruits of all your crops." (B) *What are your living expenses?* Luke 14:28

gives an appropriate analogy that emphasizes the need to determine if you have enough to spend: "Suppose one of you wants to build a tower. Will he not first sit down and estimate the cost to see if he has enough money to complete it?" (C) *Are you able to pay your debts?* Psalm 37:21 reminds us to pay our debts: "The wicked borrow and do not repay, but the righteous give generously." (D) *Are you paying your taxes?* Romans 13:7 says, "Give everyone what you owe him: If you owe taxes, pay taxes; if revenue, then revenue; if respect, then respect; if honor, then honor." (E) *Are you saving?* Proverbs 21:20 says, "In the house of the wise are stores of choice food and oil, but a foolish man devours all he has."

Long-term financial objectives should include the following: (A) *College funding:* "Children should not have to save up for their parents, but parents for their children" (2 Corinthians 12:14); (B) *freedom from debt:* part of your plan should be freedom from financial bondage; (C) *retirement:* being able to have a source of retirement income; (D) *financial independence:* being able to leave a lasting financial legacy; and (E) *charitable giving:* Proverbs 19:17 reminds us, "He who is kind to the poor lends to the Lord, and he will reward him for what he has done."

The following are procedures to follow in setting up a financial plan. Determine and summarize your present financial situation; establish short- and long-term financial objectives; create a plan by evaluating your income and expenses; create a financial strategy; implement your plan and stick to it; then review and evaluate your financial plan for major changes. Always pray.

According to Ron Blue, the following are Biblical principles for having a successful financial plan: (1) *Believe that God owns it all.* Psalm 24:1 reminds us that "the earth is the Lord's and everything in it, the world, and all who live in it." (2) *Spend less than you earn.* Proverbs 13:11 says, "Dishonest money dwindles away, but he who gathers money little by little makes it grow." (3) *Build liquidity and reserve.* Proverbs 6:6-8 gives us this analogy: "Go to the ant, you sluggard, consider its ways and be wise. It has no commander, no overseer, or ruler, yet it stores its provisions in summer and gathers its food at harvest." (4) *Avoid the use of debt.* Proverbs 22:7 says, "The rich rule over the poor and the borrower is servant to the lender." (5) *Set long-term goals.* Proverbs 16:9 says, "In his heart a man plans his course, but the Lord determines his steps."

God is the owner of all things. Again, Psalm 24:1 says, "The earth is the Lord's, and everything in it, the world, and all who live in it." Job 1:21 also says, "Naked I came from my mother's womb, and naked I will depart. The Lord gave and the Lord has taken away; may the name of the Lord be praised." In life application, do we believe this truth in theory but deny it in practice?

We are God's stewards. 2 Corinthians 9:7 says, "Each man should give what he has decided in his heart to give, not reluctantly or under compulsion, for God loves a cheerful giver." In life application, do we spend enough time on the priorities in our lives? Are we useful to God, according to our abilities and talents? Do we portray a balanced lifestyle? How are we teaching our children with the knowledge of God's Word?

What is the role of money in your life? First Timothy 6:10 says, "For the love of money is a root of all kinds of evil. Some people, eager for money, have wandered from the faith and pierced themselves with many griefs." Money is a financial tool we use to accomplish the desires we have in life. It is not just a tool; it is also a test of our behavior and true character. According to Billy Graham, a man's heart is closer to his wallet than almost anything else. Money management reveals the priority of our hearts and our spiritual maturity. If you really want true spiritual riches, you must faithfully manage money, for as Luke 16:11 says, "If you have not been trustworthy in handling worldly wealth, who will trust you with true riches?" Your heart reveals your true treasures, for "where your treasure is, there your heart will be also" (Matthew 6:21). Ask yourself the following personal questions: What does my money management tell me about my walk with Christ? How is my manner of managing money different from the unsaved? If we falter in this area, as in any area, all we have to do is humbly approach our heavenly Father in prayer and come to Him with our faults and our sins. He will lovingly receive us with open arms.

To get our finances in order, we must have a spending plan. Moreover, we also want to familiarize ourselves with some financial concerns and how they affect us financially, such as budgeting, borrowing and debts, saving and investing, bankruptcy, and retirement challenges.

*Budgeting.* Proverbs 21:5 says, "The plans of the diligent lead to profit as surely as haste to poverty." In order to create a monthly budget, you must consider getting everyone's involvement in setting targets so that each person will see the value in the limits you want to set. Then you must stick to your budget, review your spending, and always pray.

*Borrowing and Debts.* Proverbs 22:7 says, "The rich rule over the poor and the borrower is servant to the lender." Debt is not a sin, but it can become a real danger when there is greed, self-indulgence, or lack of self-discipline. There are also the economic and spiritual dangers. Economically, the principle of compounding interest will work against you. That debt becomes a trap, and debt always mortgages the future. Spiritually, borrowing always presumes the future. But James 4:16 says that presuming upon future is arrogance. It is boasting and bragging, and "all such boasting is evil." Borrowing may deny God an opportunity to work. We are in a sense putting the lender in the place of God. Sometimes we are impatient. We are unwilling to wait for God's timing to meet our needs and instead seek to meet our needs and desires in our own way and timing.

*Investments.* Proverbs 6:6-8 says, "Go to the ant, you sluggard, consider its ways and be wise; it has no commander, no overseer, or ruler, yet it stores its provisions in summer and gathers its food at harvest." Investment is one of the ways to accumulate wealth. There are factors to consider before investing, however. Given the right motives to invest, one must consider his or her present financial situation, financial goals and objectives, age, and whether one is a conservative or aggressive investor. Proverbs 21:5 says, "The plans of the diligent lead to profit as surely as haste leads to poverty." And Proverbs 21:20 says, "In the house of the wise are stores of choice food and oil, but a foolish man devours all he has." In Ecclesiastes 11:2, we read, "Give portions to seven, yes to eight, for you do not know what disaster may come upon the land."

*Bankruptcy.* In Isaiah 43:2-3, the Lord says, "When you pass through the waters, I will be with you, and when you pass through the rivers, they will not sweep over you. When you walk through the fire, you will not be burned; the flames will not set you ablaze, for I am your Lord, and God." Bankruptcy may be used in certain situations to effectively provide equitable treatment for all personal creditors, but it should not be seen as a way to avoid repaying lenders. A believer should repay whatever he owes. Proverbs 22:26-27 says, "Do not be a man who strikes hands in pledge or puts up security for debts; if you lack the means to pay, your very bed will be snatched from under you." Romans 13:8 also says, "Let no debt remain outstanding, except the continuing debt to love one another, for he who loves his fellowman has fulfilled the law." Psalm 37:21 says, "The wicked borrow and do not repay, but the righteous give generously."

*Retirement Challenges.* The most common retirement challenges are: longevity, high cost of medical expenses, and the uncertainty of the economy. Investment risk, inflation risk, and market risk relate to the volatility of the market that is now impacting our 401Ks, IRAs, and pensions. Housing foreclosures, high cost of living, and government and political agendas are highly impacting us on both a personal level and an economic level.

Here on earth, we are judged by what we do. But with God, we are judged by what is in our hearts. God looks at our hearts and not our accomplishments. What did you do with what you received from God? Is your heart for the things of the world or the things of God? As a financial advisor, it was easy to pick a subject for my Bible study class. Living a balanced financial life was our very first topic. Driven by the current financial crisis, this topic was very timely and very appropriate for the class. There was much learning delivered to the group that enabled everyone to gain in-depth knowledge into living a balanced financial life. Through this study, our group strived to discover God's truth about money and important Biblical concepts and to apply this wisdom to our lives and, ultimately, to share this truth with others. During the process, I met people who were already facing financial dilemma. We therefore prayed together and asked direction from our Father.

As I began to personally seek God's truth about money and possessions, I came to realize that I faltered in some ways. I thought I was making a significant contribution to myself and my family by working hard to save money for my children's future and for our retirement. Little did I know that I was also deviating from God's plan for my life. I began to acquire real estate properties, hoping to create a comfortable lifestyle for my family. At first, I thought I was good at it, and surely I was; but with the downturn of the economy I realized what a big mistake I had made in positioning myself this way financially. People like me, like many of us, could be easily swayed by the many choices of economic opportunities. As I was experiencing this challenge and as I was seeing and dealing with even worse financial dilemmas of friends and clients, my heart became burdened.

It did not come easily for me to deal with clients' financial challenges, especially when they got so frustrated they started to cry. All I ended up telling them was to trust in the Lord. All I could do was to pray for them. If they did not know the Lord, I began to share with them about God's love and plan for mankind. Such a difficult time may be the opportunity for them to come to God and start a relationship with Him. My heart's desire is for God to use me as an instrument to make a difference in the lives of others, especially in their relationship with God.

***Heavenly Father:***

*For what we have done to our lives*
*There is no excuse.*
*Please forgive us.*

*For we were quick to respond to our earthly desires,*
*Yet we were slow to respond to Your godly desires.*
*Please help us.*

*For our eyes were blinded by arrogance*
*And our hearts hardened by pride.*
*Please guide us.*

*And we were busy chasing after earthly purpose.*
*But only in You, Father, do we find our true purpose.*
*Please direct us*

*To a life everlasting. AMEN.*

***Personal Reflection (Financial—Wealth):***

- Are you living a balanced financial life?
- What are your financial worries?

- Do you have a testimony related to God's principles for money?
- Write your personal prayer.

## *Physical—Health*

First Corinthians 6:19-20 says, "Do you not know that your body is a temple of the Holy Spirit, who is in you, whom you have received from God? You are not your own, you were bought at a price. Therefore, honor God with your body."

When I turned fifty a few years ago, I began to notice a lot of changes in my physical body and well-being. I kept reminding myself to exercise and to watch my diet, but the reminders soon slipped away. But lately, almost every morning when I wake up, I feel sluggish and lousy. I am no longer able to do many of the things I once enjoyed doing, like gardening, cleaning, and decorating my house. In my medicine cabinet are more stacks of medicines than ever. "Why don't I feel good?" seems to be the question I often ask myself every morning. I have noticed that sometimes on days I didn't feel good I became less focused and my energy level went down. I lost my enthusiasm for that day's activities, especially my work, and that was not very becoming of me. Lately I have begun to get tired quickly and easily. Could these be my red flags?

I never realized until recently that my body is beginning to catch up with me in response to the environment I created during my younger years. I always lived a fast-phased, hardworking, overindulgent lifestyle, which I believe consumed my physical and emotional resources. I was the type of person who did not believe in idle time. I made sure that I was always productive. I was always full of creative ideas on how to be this or that. It became a way of life for me.

I have to admit that I failed to follow God's command to honor Him with my body. Henceforth, I need to examine myself to be sure I am not being spiritually double-minded.

Am I believing one thing about God's command and doing another? Perhaps this will now be the moment to recommit myself to the Lord, to ask His forgiveness as I begin to make choices that will help me stay in the right relationship with God. Honoring God with my body, beyond merely talking about getting a good healthy diet and exercise, not only helps me feel good but also creates in me a healthy relationship with God.

In Luke 11:34-36, Jesus said,

> Your eye is the lamp of your body. When your eyes are good, your whole body also is full of light. But when they are bad, your body also is full of darkness. See to it, then that the light within you is not darkness. Therefore, if your whole body is full of light and no part of it dark, it will be completely lighted, as when the light of a lamp shines on you.

It is my conviction that by faithfully obeying God's Word we can create an environment for both our mind and body that will help promote healthy and godly living as we journey heavenward.

***Heavenly Father:***

*Your words that our body is the temple of the Holy Spirit*
*Just agonized me in the way I took care of mine.*
*I was overworked, emotionally drained, and overindulged with food.*
*Please forgive me and have mercy on me.*
*I will cry 'til the break of the dawn as I say, "Please forgive me."*
*I kneel and bow down, weeping again as I say, "Please forgive me."*
*How much longer I would keep on crying and weeping*
*Just for you to hear how truly so sorry I am. AMEN.*

***Personal Reflection (Physical—Health):***

- What is your conviction, if any, concerning your physical body?
- How is your health?
- Write your personal prayer.

## *Emotional—Mind and Thoughts*

Out of your mouth comes the meditation of your heart. Words that edify lift up the spirit, but words that destroy pierce your heart. Too often, as James 3:10 says, "Out of the same mouth come praise and cursing."

My husband loves to make jokes, and often he needs to be reminded, "If you don't have anything good to say about people, don't even open your mouth." The tongue is very powerful. James 3:9 says, "With the tongue, we praise our Lord and Father, and with it we curse men, who have been made in God's likeness." Therefore, we have to be watchful for every word that comes out of our mouth.

Dr. Betty Albritton, a very dear friend of mine, is a member of the organizing committee of the STEM (Science, Technology, Engineering, and Math) Program. The program is designed to encourage young women of color in grades 5 through 10 to continue their education in the stated areas, which are underserved by women in the workforce. Once a year, usually the first Saturday in May, the organization holds a seminar primarily to mentor these children. Speakers and educators from different fields of expertise come to share their inspiring messages and learning tools with these children. I happen to be one of the presenters. Speaking to these children about their dreams and goals fascinates them more than the information I give them on finance. When they are asked what they want to be or what they plan to do in the future, you can see their eyes light up. You can feel the vibrant enthusiasm they portray as they speak up.

People are more likely to respond when we reach out to them through their hearts rather than their minds. This has been my most rewarding experience as a financial advisor. My clients always interact well with sincerity and honesty. In fact, the business philosophy I came up with is this: To build a lifelong relationship with clients based on mutual trust and honesty, thus providing high quality personalized financial services in a friendly environment.

Our emotions and our innermost feelings are crucial to our reactions. Jesus said, "Love the Lord your God with all your heart and with all your soul and with all your mind" (Matthew 22:37). I certainly believe that if you love the Lord, it carries with it your mind, body, and soul.

Everything we feed our minds influences our emotions. Psalm 19:14 says, "May the words of my mouth and the meditation of my heart be pleasing in your sight, O Lord, my Rock and my Redeemer." Our minds have the power to change our behavior; therefore, we have to guard our minds from the corrupting influence of our environment.

While I was growing up, I was determined to make the best of myself in all facets of life. I set my mind to all my plans. Growing up in a small town in the Philippines without electricity, it seems unimaginable to think that I now live in a very privileged country with a very privileged lifestyle. What I envisioned for myself as a child was to become the best person I could ever be—dedicated, hardworking, finishing college and grabbing every good and honest opportunity that came my way, and always learning. It surely happened. Coming to America was not part of the plan. I am grateful and thankful to God for giving me my husband, Rey, who gave me the opportunity to immigrate to the U.S. God, in His mighty power, paved my way to a much better place to live with my future family. I utilized every opportunity I had to improve my standard of living. I got a good job for a utility company, which enabled my husband and me to buy our first house. My children are gifts from God, I must say. Trisha and Karina both did well in school, even as I went back to school to continue my studies further. We all graduated successfully. Finishing my graduate program led me to a better career opportunity where I found my real calling. Working with people gave me the most rewarding career as it expanded my opportunities to fully utilize my God-given resources. My career was further enhanced by the conviction that my practice was His purpose, as I proclaimed God. Today, I am passionately determined to dedicate my life and my career to God Almighty, as I have been convicted to fully submit myself to Him as He leads me on a journey heavenward. I have found my real calling, and part of that calling is this book.

***Heavenly Father:***

*Teach us to say the words that edify*
*For Your kingdom to be magnified.*
*Teach us to do the things that are worthy*
*For Your purpose to be glorified.*
*As we become watchful of the things we say,*
*We also become sensitive to the things we do*
*In proclaiming peace, love, and joy*
*To all men, women, and children around us. AMEN.*

***Personal Reflection (Emotional—Mind and Thoughts):***

- What are your thoughts regarding the statement, "Our minds have the power to change our behavior; therefore, we have to guard our minds from the corrupting influence of our environment?"
- Do you have a testimony concerning your mind and thoughts?
- Write your personal prayer.

***

## *Chapter Five*

# CALL TO GODLY VIRTUES

It is very reassuring to be reminded of what is said in 1 Corinthians 13:13: "And now these three remain: faith, hope, and love. But the greatest of these is love."

**F A I T H** - **F**ather **A**s **I** **T**ruly **H**onor
Thy Holiness
**H O P E** - **H**eaven **O**ffers **P**erfect **E**ntry
Through grace and mercy
**L O V E** - **L**ord **O**f **V**ictory **E**nthroned
By God Almighty

> God will give each person according to what he has done. (Romans 2:6)

### *Love*

Jesus said in Matthew 22:37-39, "Love the Lord your God with all your heart and with all your soul and with all your mind. This is the first and greatest commandment. And the second is like it: 'Love your neighbor as yourself.'"

In Mathew 5:44-45, He said, "But I tell you: Love your enemies and pray for those who persecute you that you may be sons of your Father in heaven." And 1 Corinthians 13:4-8 says,

> Love is patient, love is kind. It does not envy, it does not boast, it is not proud. It is not rude, it is not self-seeking, it is not easily angered, it keeps no record of wrongs. Love does not delight in evil but rejoices with

> the truth. It always protects, always trusts, always hopes, always perseveres. Love never fails. But where there are prophecies, they will cease, where there are tongues, they may be stilled, where there is knowledge, it will pass away.

Love—the kind of love that only God can bring—endures forever. Our love for each other is nothing compared to the love of God.

My husband and I have been married for almost thirty years now. In spite of all the trials we've gone through, our love for each other was the biggest factor that kept our relationship alive. Sometimes it was hard for me to define the true meaning of love as I related to the demands of life. Torn between daily activities, career, children, parents, and relatives, it was hard to comprehend. But over time, just taking one day at a time and one step at a time brought us forward to a new beginning, a new perspective, and a new concept. Coming to the Lord marked a new beginning that strengthened our relationship which had almost faded away. Allowing God to intervene in our love created sparks that indeed reignited the passion and, ultimately, unleashed God's blessings.

***Heavenly Father**:*

*Your Love endures forever.*
*Great is Your faithfulness.*
*I adore and thank You. AMEN.*

***Personal Reflection (Love)**:*

- Is there any significant experience in your life that can relate to this topic?
- What is your conviction regarding love?
- Write your personal prayer.

## *Faith*

Hebrews 11:6 says, "And without faith it is impossible to please God, because anyone who comes to him must believe that he exists and that he rewards those who earnestly seek Him." This Scripture shows us the essential elements of faith. First, ***we want to know God***. Knowing God as our Savior and our Lord is the first element of faith. Through faith, we earnestly seek greater understanding of God. Second, ***we trust God***. Trusting Him is the second element of faith. It is believing in our heart that God is real. Our experience and daily provision will testify that God exists. Therefore, by our faith we trust and rely on God. Third, ***we follow God's command***. After we know and believe that God is real, then we follow Him; this is the third element of faith. We do the things He wants us to do; we please God and experience His love. Through faith, we become obedient and faithful to His command. Paul wrote to the Colossians, "For though I am absent from you in body, I am present with you in spirit and delight to see how orderly you are and how firm your faith in Christ is." (Colossians 2:5). Through our prayers, we ask God for the spirit of wisdom and revelation to know Him more. Knowing Him more opens the truth that will set us free. In 2 Corinthians 5:6-7, Paul further states, "Therefore we are always confident and know that as long as we are at home in the body we are away from the Lord. We live by faith, not by sight."

On many occasions I have had experiences that affirmed my faith in the Lord. Earnestly seeking God, trusting Him, and being obedient to Him meant that my involvement in God's work occupied a large portion of my schedule. Time spent at my regular job immensely decreased, but I was determined to focus on my writing. Sundays must be devoted to God, and most of my evenings were spent writing this book. What Jesus said in Matthew 6:33 became a faithful promise in my life: "But seek first his kingdom and his righteousness, and all these things will be given to you as well." Indeed, my Father in heaven provided everything I needed. He gave me business and provided me with resources for my financial needs. Never will I again worry for quite some time. As I was writing this book, many more things happened that solemnly declared that my Father in heaven was providing beyond what money can give, thus assuring me that this was the best decision I have ever made in my life. It further transformed my life perspectives and my husband's as well. Again, my faith was reignited with the truth of John 14:11-13: "Believe me when I say that I am in the Father and the Father is in me; or at least believe on the evidence of the miracles themselves. I tell you the truth, anyone who has faith in me will do what I have been doing. He will do even greater things than these, because I am going to the Father. And I will do whatever you ask in my name, so that the Son may bring glory to the Father."

Jesus Christ's death on the cross portrayed the greatest example of faith. His pain and suffering for our redemption was the most sacrificial offering anyone can give. Washing away our sins by the shedding of the blood of Jesus would significantly remind us that God is our true great Redeemer.

The following are Scriptures on the subject of Faith versus Fear.

> So do not fear, for I am with you; do not be dismayed, for I am your God. I will strengthen you and help you; I will uphold you with my righteous right hand. (Isaiah 41:10)

> For God has not given us a spirit of timidity, but a spirit of power, of love and of self-discipline. (2 Timothy 1:7)

> Command those who are rich in this present world not to be arrogant nor to put their hope in wealth, which is

so uncertain, but to put their hope in God, who richly provides us with everything for our enjoyment. (1 Timothy 6:17)

***Heavenly Father***:

*Seeking Your understanding,*
*We come to know You.*
*Believing You in our hearts,*
*We learn to love You.*
*Obeying Your promises,*
*We have faith in You,*
*Faith that makes us:*
*Sure of what we hope for,*
*Certain of what we do not see.* AMEN.

***Personal Reflection (Faith)***:

- Do you have a testimony of faith?
- What is your conviction?
- Write your personal prayer.

## *Hope*

Difficult times do come, and it becomes quite easy to be discouraged and defeated. Sometimes we prefer to be alone and away from people to escape the reality. There are times we want to give up life. Where is God in all of this? With the recent economic uncertainty, this is the question of many. Often we like to put the blame on somebody else for our circumstances rather than taking the responsibility ourselves. Instead of seeking help to alleviate the pain and suffering, we end up hurting more people. It is not easy at all to handle or overcome difficult situations. But Romans 8:24-25 puts it this way: "For in this hope we were saved. But hope that is seen is no hope at all. Who hopes for what he already has? But if we hope for what we do not yet have, we wait for it patiently." Hope indeed is what we need the most—hope that will bring light to the future and hope that will enlighten our perspectives. Lamentations 3:25 says, "The Lord is good to those whose hope is in him, to the one who seeks him." Only through God can we find hope that gives us courage, confidence, contentment, and comfort. We hear people say, "Time will heal," but it is not time alone that heals but rather, over time, hope brings assurance and a clear realization of God's promise. For some, that means physical healing.

This was very true in the case of my dearest friends Ed and Aida. Her testimony presented below is in her own words. She hopes that, through her testimony, she can bless people and send the message that God heals (Jehovah Rophe) and that God provides for all our needs (Jehovah Jireh.)

*It was September 7, 2005, when I was diagnosed with a nasal pharyngeal cancer. It was also the month when my husband lost his job due to downsizing. Both of my sons did not have jobs at the time, and neither did my brother who had just come from the Philippines and was staying with us. Altogether, there were five of us in our household, and none of us was working.*

*On September 7, 2005, I had surgery for a lymph node biopsy, and on September 18, 2005, I had another surgery to put a tube in my ear. On September 19, 2005, my mother-in-law passed away, and a month later, my brother-in-law passed away as well. So many things were going on at the time, and as the old cliché says, when it rains, it pours. But thanks be to God, He was always there to uphold us.*

*The treatment plan for me was seven weeks, or thirty-five days, of radiation treatment. Before I could even start the treatment, two things had to be done. First was to put the feeding tube (in my stomach) in place since, as the radiation progressed, I wouldn't be able to eat through my mouth. Second was to have fluoride treatment trays made. Fluoride treatment should be performed every night because radiation will cause dry mouth, and cavities, in turn, would destroy my teeth.*

*I told my radiologist, Dr. Damon Smith, that we did not have dental insurance due to the loss of our jobs. He told me he could not start the treatment until these two things were in place. He gave me a calling card and told me to call this dentist, Dr. Dave Tagge, and so I did. Dr. Tagge gave me a full mouth X-ray, made fluoride trays for the fluoride treatments, and gave me fluoride gels and monthly checkups and fluoride treatments in his clinic for five months. And all I paid for all his services and dental supplies was $70. I do not think it was a mere coincidence that someone did all that for me. God works in mysterious ways. It was the Lord who made this possible. Praise be to God!*

*Before I was able to start the radiation treatment, I went through a lot of blood tests, an MRI scan, and a PET scan. December 8 was my first radiation. I felt so anxious that day. I did not know what to expect. The radiation itself was painless and just fifteen minutes each time. I went Monday through Friday for seven weeks. As the radiation progressed, the effects became evident— loss of voice, loss of hair close to the neck, loss of appetite, ulceration of the mouth and throat, loss of energy, loss of taste, dry mouth, fatigue, and weight loss.*

*The process was slow, and I felt it was taking too long to complete the treatment. I was struggling with the pain and being helpless. There were nights I could not sleep, and I cried. Nights like that became prayer nights. I was not mad at God and did not question God about the cancer. Somehow, deep in my heart, I knew God was going to see me through. Ed and I had the peace of God as we went through the trials.*

*God was with me from the beginning to the end of the ordeal. I was not alone, and I lacked nothing. God supplied all my needs according to His riches in glory. I had tremendous support from my loved ones, my church family, relatives, and friends like you who so lovingly upheld me in prayers. It was these prayers that made something so difficult, bearable.*

*God even gave me an assurance that I would be fine. And this happened during our Thanksgiving celebration service in church, when there was a heavy anointing of the Holy Spirit during the service. The Holy Spirit spoke through two of our young people to let me know that I would be fine.*

*God is still in the business of answering prayers. I was healed through the prayers of many, and I am here to testify of His goodness. God still does miracles.*

*There is a reason behind everything, even when my husband got laid off from work. God knew that I needed him. It was God's purpose to have Ed by my side to take care of my needs. Ed became a driver, caregiver, encourager, moral support, prayer partner, friend, among many other things. It would have been very difficult without him by my side.*

*God's timing is perfect. When the treatment was finished and I was strong enough to drive, move around, and do things, the Lord gave Ed a job. This job paid a lot more than his previous job. Isn't God good? He restored my husband's job and gave him even a better job. God is a God of restoration. He healed me and restored my health.*

*I thank God for Pastor Wilson and Sis Lydia for lifting me up in prayers, for all the brothers and sisters in Christ, relatives and friends like you, for the untiring support and love. I am grateful for the cards, flowers, books, CD, blanket, phone calls, food, and, most of all, the love and the encouraging words. There were times when the budget was low and God would surprise us with monetary love gifts from friends and church members. Even before we asked, the Lord already knew what we needed. We lacked nothing because of God's provision. The Lord truly is Jehovah Jireh.*

Romans 5:3-4 says, "Not only so, but we also rejoice in our sufferings, because we know that suffering produces perseverance; perseverance, character; and character, hope." HOPE means **H**e **O**ffers **P**erfect **E**ndurance that will build courage and strength.

***Heavenly Father, I pray that:***

*When difficult times do come,*
*It is not because of what we have done,*
*Pain and suffering could surely harm,*
*But God's love alleviate all with an open arm. AMEN.*

***Heavenly Father:***

*Open our eyes and ears to the facts of life*
*To distinguish between real and unreal,*

*To determine light and darkness,*
*To separate the good and the bad.*

***Help us Father*:**
*Not to have fear but to have faith,*
*Not to harbor anger but to forgive,*
*Not to hate but to love,*
*For You, God, give Faith, Hope, and Love. AMEN.*

***Personal Reflection (Hope)*:**

- Do you have a testimony that relates to the topic?
- What is your conviction regarding hope?
- Write your personal prayer.

***

## *Chapter Six*

# COMMITMENT TO CHARACTER DEVELOPMENT

> But the fruit of the Spirit is love, joy, peace, patience, kindness, goodness, faithfulness, gentleness and self-control. Against such things there is no law. (Galatians 5:22-23)

Most of our character is established early in life, influenced by our family and other significant people during childhood. We also develop character by going through adversity. This is attested in Romans 5:3-4: "Not only so, but we also rejoice in our sufferings, because we know that suffering produces perseverance; perseverance, character; and character, hope." Based on experience, the radical change in my basic character came later in life when I came to know my Savior and my Lord and began to establish a growing relationship with Jesus Christ. Let us look, then, at some of the basic elements of Christian character.

## *Righteousness*

In Matthew 5:6, Jesus said, "Blessed are those who hunger and thirst for righteousness, for they will be filled." Psalm 15:1-2 also states, "Lord, who may dwell in your sanctuary? Who may live on your holy hill? He whose walk is blameless and who does what is righteous, who speaks the truth from his heart." Being righteous is being morally upright in your thoughts, words, and deeds. Romans 1:17 says, " For in the gospel a righteousness from God is revealed, a righteousness that is by faith from first to last, just as it is written: The righteous will live by faith." Without faith, there is no righteousness from God. This is confirmed in Romans 3:22: "This righteousness from God comes through faith in Jesus Christ to all who believe. There is no difference." Greater blessing comes to those who suffer because of their righteousness, as Matthew 5:10 says: "Blessed are those who are persecuted because of righteousness, for theirs is the kingdom of heaven."

We must always be guided by our good moral conduct as we continue to seek God in our journey to His kingdom.

***Heavenly Father:***

*You said in Your Word,*
*Blessed are those who hunger and thirst for righteousness;*
*For they will be filled.*
*Blessed are those who are persecuted because of righteousness,*
*For theirs is the kingdom of heaven. AMEN.*

***Personal Reflection (Righteousness):***

- Write your personal prayer on the subject of righteousness.

## *Forgiveness / Repentance*

A lingering weight I carried from my past continued to bring pain and suffering into my life until I learned how to forgive. The suffering and the sin that it bred was so overpowering that, in my thoughts, no one could eliminate them. The pain being inflicted by the sin seemed to prevail, and the suffering was so powerful and great that it continued to hit me in unexpected moments like a violent wind on a stormy day. This experience was real, and for a very long period of time, it became increasingly unbearable. Conceived by the feeling of distrust, anger, frustration, and fear, the pain became more excruciating. The world seemed to crush every bone in my body. I just wanted to be alone, crying and pleading to God, "Why is this happening to me?" I kept asking myself, "Where did I go wrong?"

I began to search for an answer but to no avail. It was only when I came to know the Lord that I began to notice that there was hope to relieve the pain and suffering. I prayed and meditated on God's Word as I claimed the promise in Matthew 6:14: "For if you forgive men when they sin against you, your heavenly Father will also forgive you." Over time, I was able to let go of the bondage that had held me back for a number of years, and I was able to move forward in life. I claimed God's power to forgive and the freedom of forgiveness. Jesus told Paul, "I am sending you to [the Gentiles] to open their eyes and turn them from darkness to light, and from the power of Satan to God, so that they may receive forgiveness of sins and a place among those who are sanctified by faith in me" (Acts 26:17-18). When we forgive, we are inviting God to start working in our lives. Thus, forgiveness is an act of surrender to God. We need to fully forgive from our hearts in order to make a way for our healing to begin.

Luke 13:5 says, "I tell you, no! But unless you repent, you too will all perish."

***Heavenly Father****:*

*Today I realized what I should have done*
*Long before the damage was done,*
*Holding back anger, frustration, and distrust.*
*Please forgive me, and let me learn to trust.*

*Today I must repent and learn to forgive,*
*Letting go of bondage, so You will relieve.*
*The power to forgive is truly divine.*
*Thank You, Father, for I am surely fine. AMEN.*

***Personal Reflection (Forgiveness and Repentance):***

- Write your personal prayer on the subject of forgiveness and repentance.

## *Truthfulness / Honesty / Transparency*

Do you think we grow in character in times of apparent success? It is very unlikely. In fact, from what I have seen and observed, our success can even cause us to drift away from God. We continue to develop our character more through setbacks and failures than through success. Think of it. When we experience fear, trouble, sickness, death, calamities, or any kind of dilemma, the first thing we do is pray to God and seek His guidance. But what happens when we experience life in our comfort zone? Is God as much a part of our lives then?

In John 3:16-21, Jesus said,

> For God so loved the world that he gave his one and only Son, that whoever believes in him shall not perish but have eternal life. For God did not send his Son into the world to condemn the world, but to save the world through him. Whoever believes in him is not condemned, but whoever does not believe stands condemned already because he has not believed in the name of God's one and only Son. This is the verdict: Light has come into the world, but men loved darkness instead of light because their deeds were evil. Everyone who does evil hates the light, and will not come into the light for fear that his deeds will be exposed. But whoever lives by the truth comes into the light, so that it may be seen plainly that what he has done has been done through God.

It is my conviction that light is a reflection of truth.

Everything in God's kingdom is absolute truthfulness. God wants every one of us to possess truth, as stated in Psalm 51:6: "Surely you desire truth in the inner parts; you teach me wisdom in the inmost place." Proverbs 12:22 also states, "The Lord detests lying lips, but he delights in men who are truthful." Being truthful carries with it honesty, integrity, and trustworthiness. In 2 Kings 12:15, it is said with regard to the repair of the temple, "They did not require an accounting from those to whom they gave the money to pay the workers, because they acted with complete honesty." In truth, there is transparency; there is openness and there is mutual sharing with those who are willing to humble themselves and come to God in the obedience of faith. Sin, however, leads to pretense, a lack of transparency, and a desire to be served rather than to serve. Walking in God's light leads to truthfulness and a desire to love and serve others. If we become consistent in speaking the truth, this sets us free from the burden of hidden sin. It is always necessary to maintain truthfulness and transparency for our actions, thoughts, words, and deeds to reflect our true accountability to God.

***Heavenly Father:***

*We must all be guided by the truth,*
*Truth about Your kingdom pursuit.*
*Truthfulness, transparency, and honesty*
*Will surely light up kingdom authority.*

*Lying lips and deceitful tongues*
*Lead to sin and ungodly ways;*
*But in God's absolute truthfulness*
*Is light that radiates transparency. AMEN.*

***Personal Reflection (Truthfulness, Honesty, Transparency):***

- Write your personal prayer on the subject of truthfulness, honesty, and transparency.

## *Trustworthiness*

Being a financial advisor is a big responsibility. It requires trustworthiness. In every relationship—marital, business, family—trust is critical because it creates the basic foundation. One of the essential components of our faith in God is trusting in Him. The others are acknowledging Him as our Savior and acting in obedience to Him. In Luke 16:10-12, Jesus said,

> Whoever can be trusted with very little can also be trusted with much and whoever is dishonest with very little will also be dishonest with much. So if you have not been trustworthy in handling worldly wealth, who will trust you with true riches? And if you have not been trustworthy with someone else's property, who will give you property of your own?

Scripture is trustworthy. It is reliable, credible, and accurate. It is the source of God's commands and our guide for everyday living. As we embrace trustworthiness in our daily walk, God allows us to do what is good and pleasing to Him. We must pray according to

***Psalm 25:4-6:***

*Show me your ways, O Lord,*
*teach me your paths;*
*guide me in your truth and teach me,*
*for you are God my Savior,*
*and my hope is in you all day long. AMEN.*

***Personal Reflection (Trustworthiness):***

- Write your personal prayer on the subject of trustworthiness.

## *Faithfulness*

Psalm 85:10-11 says, "Love and faithfulness meet together; righteousness and peace kiss each other. Faithfulness springs forth from the earth, and righteousness looks down from heaven." Faithfulness is adhering to God and His covenant. We have to be submissively loyal to God, unquestionably obedient to His will, sincerely devoted to Him, and lovingly true to God. We can depend on God's promises because He is reliable, truthful, and solid. God's Word is true yesterday, today, and forever.

Our faith is our confidence that brings hope to God's wondrous creation. The faithfulness of God is beyond compare, everlasting and great. Lamentations 3:22-23 says, "Because of the Lord's great love we are not consumed, for his compassions never fail. They are new every morning; great is your faithfulness." If we allow God to live in us, the Holy Spirit who dwells in us will enable us to be faithful toward God. Through the Holy Spirit, we are also being empowered to become faithful to others. Thereby, amidst all the unstable world situations and the constant changes, truth will prevail. God's truth, Word, promises, and covenant remain faithful so that we too can be faithful.

God washes away our sins if we truly repent for He is faithful and just to forgive us of our sins. As we aim to develop true, faithful character, we begin to be loyal, devoted, obedient to His will, and truthful to God. Faithfulness becomes a living reality in our life.

There are many things we can do to remain faithful to God. First, we must be consistent in our prayers, reading His Word, and sharing the gospel with others. According to M. G. Collins, (Faithfulness, "Bible Study", August 1998), we can be truly faithful when we lovingly conceal the sins of others rather than gossip about them. As Christians, we must be committed to developing our character as a reflection of God's manifestation in us, making our faith a living reality in our lives so that we can produce faithfulness. We must give priority to what is said in Proverbs 3:3: "Let love and faithfulness never leave you; bind them around your neck, write them on the tablet of your heart."

***Heavenly Father:***

*I am deeply grateful for Your wonderful acts,*
*For Your promises are plentiful for kingdom impact.*
*I will sing of the mercies of the Lord forever*
*And declare Your loving-kindness more than ever.*

*Your faithfulness, Lord God, is beyond compare.*
*Your words, promises, and covenant we truly care.*
*Through our faith we become truly confident*
*To bring hope and peace with wondrous intent*

*Faithfulness is to adhere to Your throne, O God,*
*Our faith, a living reality to honor You, O God,*
*Loyal and devoted to do Your will, O God,*
*Faithfully and lovingly true to You, O God. AMEN.*

***Personal Reflection (Faithfulness):***

- Write your personal prayer on the subject of faithfulness.

## *Humility*

Humility is the foundation of God's grace as it is also a vital aspect of salvation. Until we humble ourselves to recognize our need of Christ, we cannot experience His grace and we will not receive the kingdom of God. In Matthew 5:3, Jesus spoke this beatitude: "Blessed are the poor in spirit, for theirs is the kingdom of heaven." Therefore, the first test of a true Christian is humility. Proverbs 22:4 says, "Humility and the fear of the Lord bring wealth and honor and life." Humility is the willingness to submit to the greater wisdom of the one from whom all things come. God gives us all our abilities, time, talents, and material resources as gifts. He entrusts these things to us, and we are accountable for what we do with them.

The focus of humility is not of oneself but on God. This can be attained through our study of the Word, time in prayer, and our sincere desire to have a relationship with the Lord. The key to Christian unity is to have a real sense of humility. In Philippians 2:3-4, Paul wrote, "Do nothing out of selfish ambition or vain conceit, but in humility consider others better than yourselves. Each of you should look not only to your own interests, but also to the interests of others." Being united in love for Christ who loves us makes us understand humility. Humility considers others as better than ourselves. Jesus' death on the cross for our sins is the best representation of humility. As true believers, we need to emulate Jesus' humility.

The world cannot sustain all the things we crave because we keep wanting more and more, whether it is success, fame, position, prestige, or popularity. If we are truly humble, we must remove the things that promote pride. Proverbs 11:2 says, "When pride comes, then comes disgrace, but with humility comes wisdom." Pride is the barrier between man and God.

First Peter 5:5 warns the young, "Young men, in the same way be submissive to those who are older. All of you, clothe yourselves with humility toward one another, because 'God opposes the proud but gives favor to the humble.'"

We want what we think is best for us. Sometimes we get what we want, and sometimes we don't. But either situation could create a barrier in our relationship with God. When great fortune comes to our lives, we become very subjective, thinking we could conquer the world. We can become so proud of our accomplishments that we fail to realize that these are nothing compared to what God can provide us. And if and when the world seems to go against us, we can begin to question God. We can become resentful, envious, and judgmental, even to the extreme of harming others. These are some of the cases I have seen and dealt with in my practice. Such responses to situations can became a way of life that brings a lot of discontentment, anger, frustration, and greed.

It is only when we know Jesus and allow Him to live in us and pursue His greatness that we feel real contentment and peace. He does not want us to settle for mediocrity, for His provision is above and beyond our expectations. We must therefore give ourselves to the higher calling of God, rather than trying to impress people. Walk with excellence and with dignity, for God is the source of great character. Remember, in the end, each of us will stand before the judgment of God to give account.

***Heavenly Father:***

*Take our eyes off ourselves to look to You*
*Through the study of Your words, our time in prayer,*
*And our sincere desire to have a relationship with You.*

*Take away our selfish ambition so that we can focus on You*
*Through our willingness to submit to Your greater kingdom,*
*As we clothe ourselves with humility towards one another.*
*AMEN.*

***Personal Reflection (Humility):***

- Write your personal prayer on the subject of humility.

## *Integrity*

Samuel said to all Israel, "I have listened to everything you said to me and have set a king over you" (1 Samuel 12:1). This is a reflection of how we must keep our promises. A high degree of integrity is demanded of all of us who portray ourselves as true Christians. Christianity is about a relationship with God and having Christ live in us and manifest Himself in our lives. God must be our very foundation, and Hebrews 13:8 says, "Jesus Christ is the same yesterday and today and forever." There must be a consistency between what is inside us and what is outside us. How we live and act determine our true character and the reflection of God in our lives. James 5:12 says, "Above all, my brothers, do not swear—not by heaven or by earth or by anything else. Let your 'Yes' be yes, and your 'No,' no, or you will be condemned."

We are to be people of integrity with firm, secure, and unchanging standards. Integrity requires high moral and ethical values. One of the biggest tests of our integrity is the way we handle money. Money brings out the reality in us. Integrity is a matter of commitment and living out that commitment, especially when no one is looking. It is about treating people with dignity and caring about them. It is about God's grace making us more and more in His image and likeness.

Character development in the area of integrity carries a great deal of trust and moral/ethical values. Sadly, when it comes to finances the matter of personal character often has been misunderstood, misused, and misguided.

During the course of my practice, I have come across many people who were victims of a get-rich-quick scheme. Most of the victims are people who have very little money but have good credit and have access to credit cards. Sometimes single parents are good targets. Driven mostly by the demand of our lifestyle, people become vulnerable to hoping for a big return of their money in the quickest time possible. Many people, not realizing the legality and consequences of the business deals they are getting into, fall for the trap. It is too late when they realize that these schemes are really scams. Often the victims believe the people behind the scams are people of integrity. Sometimes it is hard to believe that the same victims fall for the same trap over and over again. In fact, I have spoken to some victims who cannot even put into words why they allowed these things to happen.

In Ezekiel 33:31, we read, "My people come to you, as they usually do, and sit before you to listen to your words, but they do not put them into practice. With their mouths they express devotion, but their hearts are greedy for unjust gain." The reality is that these people are not only victims, but because they are being enticed by the lure of money into a worldly desire, they are also dethroned from the will of God in their lives. How can we escape this trap? We must surrender our lives to God by moving in God's direction to goodness, knowledge, self-control, perseverance, godliness, brotherly kindness, and then to love. If we are unproductive and want our lives to be meaningful, we need to serve God who will give us new vision, as we seek to pursue the heavenly city through our journey.

***Heavenly Father:***

*May we be guided by Your great wisdom*
*Of true and noble character,*
*Where there is a high degree of integrity*
*As we reflect Your kingdom authority.*

*May we speak of love in our hearts,*
*Moving in Your direction to goodness,*
*Knowledge, self-control, perseverance,*
*Godliness, brotherly kindness, and love. AMEN.*

***Personal Reflection (Integrity):***

- Write your personal prayer on the subject of integrity.

***

## *Chapter Seven*

# ROADBLOCKS TO A JOURNEY HEAVENWARD

## *What Is Drawing You away from God?*

### *Sin*

Anything that is not in accordance with God's law is a sin. We are each accountable to God for our actions, thoughts, words, and deeds. Deviating from God's command and law will draw us away from God and create a roadblock to our journey heavenward. As I mentioned before, there is original sin and personal sin. The original sin refers to the sin of Adam, while personal sins are the sins we individually commit. People are sinful, as Romans 3:23 says: "For all have sinned and fall short of the glory of God." This refers to the original sin. But when we receive the Lord as Savior and ask for His forgiveness for our sins, we are saved. Christ died on the cross to redeem us from all our sins.

The committing of personal sin is within our control. When we allow ourselves to do things that are not pleasing to God, we commit sin. Romans 8:8 tells us, "Those controlled by the sinful nature cannot please God." Galatians 5:19 also states, "The acts of the sinful nature are obvious: sexual immorality, impurity and debauchery." Our goal in this book is to ask God to direct us to lead a godly life, so we must guard our actions, thoughts, words, and deeds. We must pray what is said in Psalm 119:133: "Direct my footsteps according to your Word, let no sin rule over me." Be watchful of the sinful nature, because John 9:31 says, "We know that God does not listen to sinners. He listens to the godly man who does his will." When someone commits sin against you, this is what you should do, as presented in Luke 17:3-4: "So watch yourselves, if your brother sins, rebuke him, and if he repents, forgive him. If he sins against you seven times in a day, and seven times comes back to you and says, I repent, forgive him."

God wants us to recognize our sins. Although we have not committed murder or adultery, we could still find ourselves lying or worshiping false idols such as wealth or power. In so doing, we are putting distance between us and God. Beware of the work of evil regarding deception. First John 1:8-10 says,

> If we claim to be without sin, we deceive ourselves and the truth is not in us. If we confess our sins, he is faithful and just and will forgive us our sins and purify us from all unrighteousness. If we claim we have not sinned, we make him out to be a liar and his word has no place in our lives.

Once we recognize ourselves as sinners, we need to repent and ask Jesus' forgiveness. As 2 Corinthians 7:10-11 says,

> Godly sorrow brings repentance that leads to salvation and leaves no regret, but worldly sorrow brings death. See what this godly sorrow has produced in you: what earnestness, what eagerness to clear yourselves, what indignation, what alarm, what longing, what concern, what readiness to see justice done. At every point you have proved yourselves to be innocent in this matter.

When we are in trouble, sometimes we are not sure whether the trouble is God's punishment or the work of our enemy. Sometimes it is hard to comprehend. In any case it is required that we confess our sins and put our whole trust in God. Jeremiah 33:8 is God's promise of restoration: "I will cleanse them from all the sin they have committed against me and will forgive all their sins of rebellion against me."

***Heavenly Father:***

*We acknowledge that we are accountable for our actions, thoughts, words, and deeds. We ask you to direct our footsteps so that we always do what is right. Give us wisdom according to the richness of Your Word.*

*Father, if we deviate from Your commands and laws, we ask that You forgive us.*
*We recognize that we are sinners and if we commit sins against You, we ask you to forgive us. Please do not let sin rule over us; instead, give us courage, strength, and might to reject temptations as we journey heavenward to Your kingdom authority. We ask these things in Jesus' wonderful name. AMEN.*

***Personal Reflection (Sins)**:*

- Ask forgiveness from the Lord for any sins you have committed.
- Write your personal prayer regarding sin.

## *Murder*

Jesus said in Matthew 5:21, "Do not murder, and anyone who murders will be subject to judgment." God spoke in Exodus 20:13, "You shall not murder." The latter is the sixth of the Ten Commandments. We have both God's law and human law to impose judgment on anyone who murders. One thing for sure is that God is just. God's law is supreme, and His judgment outweighs them all. Although in human law there are steps to be followed before the conviction is made, sometimes the system falters. I just could not imagine how many people have been convicted of crimes they did not commit. We hear of them all the time. But there's nothing much to be said in this area; instead, our support for them should be our prayers that God will relieve the pain and suffering of these people who have been jailed but have not done anything wrong. I pray to our Father in heaven that He may use these people significantly to share God's love and mercy to one another while imprisoned. And may those that were guilty turn their lives to God and repent of all their sins.

My main purpose for this subject is to encourage us to be faithful and obedient to God's Word for it gives guidance for our daily living. God will protect you and guide you to the right path, as Proverbs 4:10-12 says: "Listen, my son, accept what I say, and the years of your life will be many. I guide you in the way of wisdom and lead you along straight paths. When you walk, your steps will not be hampered; when you run, you will not stumble."

***Heavenly Father:***

*I pray for those people who have been convicted of things they haven't done. I also pray for people who have committed murder. I hope that this will be the time for them to come to You and accept You as their Savior. In Jesus' name, AMEN.*

***Personal Reflection (Murder):***

- Pray for people you know who have committed murder.
- Pray for all the people who are imprisoned.
- Write your personal prayer.

## *Adultery*

Jesus said in Matthew 5:27-28, "Do not commit adultery. But I tell you that anyone who looks at a woman lustfully has already committed adultery with her in his heart." God spoke in Exodus 20:14, "You shall not commit adultery." This was the seventh of the Ten Commandments.

Adultery has always brought lots of misery including divorce and broken homes. Unfortunately, it has become a way of life to some. This is not just a concern for men but for women as well. My late father was an adulterous man, and that was his way of life, I suppose, because I don't recall his ever feeling sorry for what he had done. However, my husband committed adultery, and he regretted what he did. He asked God's forgiveness for what he had done. Although it was a tedious process, I also learned to forgive him, and now, together, we both walk with the Lord.

The Bible says in 1 Peter 5:8, "Be self-controlled and alert. Your enemy the devil prowls around like a roaring lion looking for someone to devour." While it is true that God has a plan for our lives, it is also true that Satan has one too. In John 10:10, Jesus said, "The thief comes only to steal and kill and destroy; I have come that they may have life, and have it to the full." And if the Evil One could take you out of God's plan, He would likely do so through human weakness, the flesh. This is why Satan's scheme often involves sexual sin. In order to fight against this weakness and its consequences, it is imperative to build a deep and intimate relationship with the Lord and with your spouse. In 1 Corinthians 6:18 Paul writes, "Flee from sexual immorality. All other sins a man commits are outside his body, but he who sins sexually sins against his own body." We must therefore do what Ecclesiastes 9:9 says: "Enjoy life with your wife, whom you love, all the days of this meaningless life that God has given you under the sun—all your meaningless days. For this is your lot in life and in your toilsome labor under the sun."

I guess I will never understand why many fall into this trap. I used to ask my husband how much of a pleasure it could bring him compared to the misery it could inflict on the family. My husband surely learned His lesson. But I lived with my father, who never learned his lesson. I also happen to know few men out there who find pleasure in committing adultery over and over again.

God made it clear that one of His greatest commandments is that which forbids adultery. How much more learning and teaching would it take for people to understand that adultery is a great sin? I agonize as I see people suffer the way I did. I wish I could do something to help them. My heart goes out to the family who suffer as victims of this sin. It is my desire to share this book with all victims of adultery, to give them hope and encouragement to come to the Lord and to forgive a sinning spouse for the wrong that one has done. Act in faith, and God will do the rest. Focus on Him in His greatness, mercy, and love. In Deuteronomy 6:4-6, the Lord says, "Hear, O Israel: The Lord our God, the Lord is one. Love the Lord your God with all your heart and with all your soul and with all your strength. These commandments that I give you today are to be upon your hearts."

***Heavenly Father:***

*I know that You have a great plan for us,*
*But I am also aware that the Evil One has, too.*
*You have come that we may have life and have it to the full,*
*But the Evil One comes only to steal and kill and destroy.*

*I pray to You, Father, that everyone will be guided by Your great commandment, "You shall not commit adultery." I also pray to You, Father, that everyone will build a deep and intimate relationship with You and with his or her spouse, that everyone will stop Satan's scheme of sexual sin. Father, I pray for everyone's direction and guidance. These things I ask in Jesus' mighty name. AMEN.*

***Personal Reflection (Adultery):***

- If Satan could take you out of God's plan, where would he most likely do it? Could it be through sex, alcohol, drugs, love of money, or power?
- Are you aware of his schemes for your life, his plan for your life?
- How healthy is your relationship with the Lord and with your spouse?
- What steps can you take to deepen your relationship with the Lord and with your spouse?
- Examine yourself to see if you're deviating from this principle of God.
- Write your personal prayer.

## *Swearing*

Jesus is quoted in Matthew 5:34-35 saying, "But I tell you, Do not swear at all: either by heaven, for it is God's throne; or by earth, for it is his footstool; or by Jerusalem, for it is the city of the Great King." It bothers me so much when I hear someone swear. Sometimes it could be a habit that people are almost unaware of. You hear people, both young and old, swear all the time, and what's more disturbing is that they swear in God's name. People's sensitivity to moral values seem diminished. I was told once that I was very old-fashioned when I commented to a young boy about his swearing. Whether it is the "in" thing or the "out" thing or whatever, I still put value in good morals. Sometimes when I hear the phrase, "go with the flow," it disappoints me because it's sending the wrong message to young people.

In the summer of 2009, I had several encounters with my nephews, who were visiting from Canada and Guam. For almost a month, I had fifteen people at my house. Five of them were my teenage nephews. They brought with them all kinds of video games and personal computers. But all their modern gadgets seemed to have replaced real connection to reality and to others. One afternoon, I happened to be in the family room with my five nephews. The room was very quiet. They were all engrossed in their electronic games and personal computers, playing their own separate games. The sad part was they were all wearing their own headsets so that no one could see or hear what the others were playing or watching. "What is wrong with this picture?" I thought. It was very sad seeing them together but with no connection to one another, sitting together but with no interaction. I was saddened by the fact that they were at my house supposedly to get together for the summer. "What happened?" I wondered. But mostly what I did not approve of was that, in some of their games or programming, there were forms of swearing, cursing, hurting, and killing. I was totally shocked, and I banned some of their choices of television programs and video games. In young people's minds, it becomes very natural for them to just say and repeat what they have heard from television and electronic games, even if it's bad. My daughters are now grown up, and it is hard for me to grasp how much luxury, freedom, and privilege young children now can have and access compared to when my daughters were young. In my living room, all that I can remember having were tons of books and a television. Times change, things change, culture changes, and moral values seemed to have been undermined. And access to media seems to have influenced innocent young minds.

It is my conviction that we should, at all times, rely on the Lord's teaching in James 5:12: "Above all, my brothers, do not swear—not by heaven or by earth or by anything else. Let your 'Yes' be yes, and your 'No,' no, or you will be condemned."

***Heavenly Father:***

*It breaks my heart to see young children becoming subdued by the influence of media like televisions, computers, and video games. They begin to lose control of their identity, even to the extreme of letting go of their moral values, because they just want to be accepted by their peers or society. Father, I pray for these young people to get direction from their parents, family, and friends who greatly love them. Children are gifts from You, Father, and I want them to know You as their Savior and Lord. There will be many changes or challenges coming their way, but, Father, with You nothing is impossible. I pray that You will be in their midst; they are young and innocent, and they need guidance. Until they find their angel to direct them, I pray that You'll be in control of their lives. This I pray in Jesus' wonderful name. AMEN.*

***Personal Reflection (Swearing):***

- Examine yourself to see if you're deviating from this principle of God.
- Set a good example to others, especially our children, by not swearing.
- Ask God to guide you to teach your children not to swear.
- Pray for guidance and direction.
- Write your personal prayer.

## *Judging Others*

Jesus said, "Do not judge, or you too will be judged for in the same way you judge others, you will be judged, and with the measure you use, it will be measured to you" (Matthew 7:1-2). It has become a way of life to many to become judgmental, to put themselves above others at the expense of others just to get what they want. Often it does not stop there; they also seem to get satisfaction from seeing people suffer from their harmful ways. This was my worst nightmare when I used to receive harassing letters that were demeaning, wicked, malicious, and harmful. Although this wicked act was done to me, it never occurred to me to wish for that person to likewise get hurt. In Luke 6:37-38, Jesus says, "Do not judge, and you will not be judged. Do not condemn and you will not be condemned. Forgive and you will be forgiven. Give and it will be given to you." If someone hurt you or harmed you, the law (people's law and God's law) is there to help you. But the power to forgive is still the best cure for someone who has been hurt or inflicted with prolonged emotional pain and suffering. The power to forgive opens enormous blessings from God. The power of forgiveness brings peace, joy, and love. Romans 14:13 says, "Therefore let us stop passing judgment on one another. Instead, make up your mind not to put any stumbling block or obstacle in your brother's way." Rather than make matters worse, obey God's command and do godly things to others, no matter what the circumstances were. God will reward you.

***Heavenly Father**:*

*No matter how grievous the circumstances are,*
*If we bring them up to Your throne, they become nothing,*
*For in You, Lord, everything is possible.*
*Wicked, malicious, demeaning, and harmful acts*
*Are simply threats from the Evil One.*
*Lead us not into retaliation, but*
*Deliver us, Lord, from evil,*
*For Your kingdom is supreme and glorious. AMEN.*

***Personal Reflection (Judging Others):***

- Present your challenges and concerns to God.
- Develop a godly habit of not judging others.
- Pray for guidance and direction.
- Pray for your enemies, learn to forgive, and be at peace with everyone.
- Write your personal prayers.

# *Idolatry*

Idolatry is putting our longings in place of God. In Colossians 3:5, God commands, "Put to death, therefore, whatever belongs to your earthly nature: sexual immorality, impurity, lust, evil desires and greed, which is idolatry." God hates idolatry because we are giving priority to other things instead of to God Himself. This is total blasphemy to our heavenly Father. Idolatry is deviating from God's purpose for mankind. God created us to glorify Him, and God wants us to delight in His glory.

With the uncertainty of the economy becoming a worldwide problem, many people are greatly concerned. We believers are almost certain that deviating from the commands and principles of godly living is the cause. The lure of material possessions led many into uncontrolled, lavish lifestyles. Hence, greed as a form of idolatry led to irreparable harm. Idolatry indeed hinders the love and trust we owe to God. Idolatry is the exact opposite of everything we're hoping to accomplish in this book. So be very careful to recognize the red flags in your walk with the Lord.

As an antidote to idolatry, we must put God at the center of our daily living. We must always seek His guidance through the hearing, reading, and studying of God's Word. We must be in constant communication with God through our daily prayers and create the habit of fellowship because we need each other's support to grow in spiritual maturity with the Lord. We are members of the same family of God. Therefore, God wants us to spread His word to all families; and how much greater value if we could share both the Word and our faith with others.

***Heavenly Father:***

*You have given us so much freedom in life,*
*Freedom that we can always turn to You*
*When things don't go right,*

*Freedom that we can also leave You*
*When everything seems all right.*
*Sometimes our freedom goes out of the way.*
*That likely could lead us to idolatry.*
*Please forgive us. Have mercy on us.*

*Today, I bow down to you, my Lord.*
*Please lead me to understand that:*
*In freedom You set me free from sins*
*When You died on the cross for my sins;*
*In freedom Your truth set me free*
*When You spoke to me through Your words.*
*Where the Spirit of the Lord is, there is freedom. AMEN.*

***Personal Reflection (Idolatry):***

- Determine the red flags (signs of idolatry) in your family. Pray for godly guidance and direction. Seek godly, professional advice.
- Ask the Lord to forgive you of any idolatrous practice.
- Ask the Lord to lead you to live a godly life.
- Write your personal prayer.

***

# *Chapter Eight*

# SOCIETAL IMPACT: CHRISTIAN PERSPECTIVES

## *Church*

Church is often viewed as the house of worship, but the church actually is a group or community of Christian believers who are responsible to encourage its members to lead a Christian life. The main focus of the church is to proclaim the message of Christianity. The leaders of the church preach the Word of God, which is a critical element in maintaining our fellowship with God and each other. All the members are encouraged to make spiritual progress and to show their faith by their actions, words, thoughts and deeds, as people who are accountable to God. Therefore, learning the Word of God is the basic foundation of faith that enables each believer to be rightly related to God. Through prayer and worship together, Christians acknowledge God's presence in their lives and express their reverence for God. In John 15:5, Jesus said, "I am the vine; you are the branches. If a man remains in me and I in him, he will bear much fruit; apart from me you can do nothing." God is the source of everything; we are His branches that must abide in Him.

Not having a clear understanding or true teaching about God was a big drawback in my earlier life. Back then, I thought of the church as a sacred place and the only place where I could commune with God. It then became my practice to go to church every Sunday, believing it was a big obligation and an opportunity to ask for God's provision. For many years, this was my customary routine. I thought that this was what life is all about. Indeed, I felt so comfortable with this that it became a way of life for me. I must have been experiencing life in what I call a "comfort zone." During those times, it never occurred to me to ask myself whether God was a big part of my life. I never asked this until I faced the biggest trial in my life.

When tragic things hit my marriage, I began to feel empty and lost. I needed direction and guidance. I sought advice from the church I was attending, but the counseling I received didn't make any sense. I was crying out for help. I did not know what to do. One day, my neighbor invited me to a church called the New Beginning Community Church. At this church, I began to see a difference. I came to learn the Biblical foundation of the Christian life and started to build my personal relationship with God. It was at this church that I received the gift of salvation and came to know Christ as my Savior and my Lord. It is my conviction that God paved the way for me to find this church which encouraged me to make spiritual progress.

I began to pray the words of Psalm 25:4: "Show me your ways, O Lord, teach me your paths." Getting involved in church activities, such as Bible studies, gave me a great reward. It helped me grow in my spiritual walk with my Father. At this church I was fed by the Word of God, learned to pray, worshiped, and found fellowship with others. As I continued further to seek for my Father in heaven, He opened an opportunity for me to move to another church. This church is called Maranatha Chapel. I have been attending this church now for more than eight years. Tremendous spiritual support has been provided for me by the church congregation and especially by the teaching of my pastor, Ray Bentley. Through this church, God enabled me to grow in spiritual maturity in my relationship with Him. I have become involved with some of the church ministries, leading a Bible study group and participating in women's ministry. I began to feel that my Father in heaven has a far greater calling for me. Thus, I must always be ready, able, and willing to serve Him.

My thoughts for people who are looking for a church are to pray and to seek a church that submits "the words of the Amen, the faithful and true witness, the ruler of God's creation" (Revelation 3:14).

***Heavenly Father*:**

*Sometimes when life seems bright, we undermine You.*
*Sometimes when life goes our own way, we ignore You.*
*Sometimes when life brings fortune, we disobey You.*
*But when life*
*seems dark and gloomy,*
*goes the opposite way,*
*misfortune overtakes our way,*
*Then quickly we ask,*
*Where are You, Father?*
*Only then we realize that it is because of You, Father, that we are alive. AMEN.*

**CHURCH**

**C**- Church is a place to worship You
**H**- Heavenly Father, so faithful and true.
**U**- Undoubtedly Your love so supreme
**R**- Redeems man of his unrighteousness.
**C**- Character You began to mold;
**H**- Humility in our hearts You now unfold.

***Personal Reflection (Church):***

- Write your personal prayer for your church.

## *Workplace*

It is said in 2 Timothy 1:7, "For God did not give us a spirit of timidity, but a spirit of power, of love and of self-discipline."

Most of us work approximately forty hours a week in our workplace. The quantity and quality of time we spend in our job, with our family, and with God all reflects our allegiance to God.

We must be good stewards of our time and abilities. Therefore, self-discipline, which is crucial in our personal life, is equally important in the workplace.

God Himself is a worker. For six days He worked. After He finished His creation, He took a day off, rested, and went back to work. In John 5:17, Jesus said, "My Father is always at his work to this very day, and I, too, am working." God's purpose for work was to benefit us so that we would have a sense of self-worth, so that we would have enhanced relationships, and so that our physical needs would be met. Ecclesiastes 3:13 tells us, "That everyone may eat and drink, and find satisfaction in all his toil—this is the gift of God."

God also created us with an emotional need that can be met only by an honest day's work. Thus, when we complete a task, no matter how difficult it might have been, we feel satisfied and valuable.

In the real world of the workplace, however, there will always be troubles. Often we have more questions than answers, more problems than solutions. Stress seems to be a daily part of our routine due to the nature of our work, the workload, and especially our coworkers. Much of the stress comes as a result of our unmet desires for recognition, power, and control. Sometimes we desperately drive ourselves to handle trials and tribulations, pushing ourselves to the end of our rope rather than seeking advice or help. We often think that we are strong enough to deal with life on our own. Little do we know that such an attitude can possibly do us far greater harm. We have to understand that, during these moments, the only thing we can do is to submit ourselves to the grace of God. We must allow God to control the situation. When we realize that God is the ultimate source of every good thing, then we can learn to trust ourselves and others and to never clutch tightly to the things of this world.

Stress at the workplace is not always the result of one's self-seeking desire for power, control, or recognition. It also can be the result of someone else's desire of power. Abuse of power can be very destructive and can affect many, many people. The same can be said for playing politics. Pride, envy, and greed that arise from sinful human nature can corrupt the workplace, resulting in continual frustration and unhealthy stress.

Where I once worked, I was under a lot of stress. I lost count of how many times I cried, not because of the nature of work, but because of the people I worked with. I guess I was overly sensitive to how things were handled at my department, and I felt victimized with unmerited performance reviews. As much as I tried to work hard, it never seemed to be up to the standard. During those years, I was working full-time and part-time and, at the same time, going to school. Although I also was having problems with my marital relationship, I did not feel that I was not performing well at work. I was always determined to perform every task as best I could. But then again, maybe I was just seeing my side of the picture. Needless to say, when I encountered several medical problems and went on sick leave, I finally decided to leave my job. Maybe I thought God had a better plan for me. I took my doctor's advice to resign because it was aggravating my physical well-being. I was very thankful to God for allowing me to reach the breaking point for my own good.

I went on to a new venture, becoming a financial advisor. I certainly could associate my new job with positive challenges, significance, and meaning. It became an opportunity to express honest, truthful, caring concern every time I met with people. My very first year in the industry was a great success because I didn't have to ever again prove how capable I was at performing my task. I can honestly say that I laid my entire burden at the workplace on God to help and guide me in my everyday tasks. I learned to trust in Him and have faith in Him. Often my colleagues asked me what was my secret. In response, I would say, "God is my secret." Only God knows my true purpose; I am just being obedient and faithful. At all times, we should rely on God's guidance and direction for our lives. I truly believe that seeking God's presence in our lives, through His Word and our faith, reveals His true purpose for us, whether it is in our personal life, our relationships with others, or even in our workplace.

***Heavenly Father***:

*Thank You for reminding us that Your intention for work was to benefit us so that we would have a sense of self-worth and enhanced relationships and our physical needs would be met. Although sometimes at the workplace pride, envy, and greed exist, I pray, Father, to please teach us that the only thing we can do is to submit ourselves to Your grace. We must learn to allow You, Father, to intervene and take control of the situation. Enable us, Father, to trust ourselves and others and never again clutch tightly to the things of this world. Provide us guidance and direction to never fall into a trap of deceptive, ungodly purpose. All this I ask in Jesus' wonderful name. AMEN.*

**WORKPLACE**

**W**-Work is for our benefit to meet our physical need,
**O**-Obedience and self-discipline being crucial indeed.
**R**-Relationship to God and to others must be truthful,
**K**-Kind, trustworthy, dedicated, and faithful.
**P**-People in the workplace can sometimes bring turmoil.
**L**-Learn to allow God's intervention to get us out of trouble.
**A**-Always remember to submit ourselves to the grace of God,
**C**-Creator of heaven and earth, our dear almighty Father,
**E**-Enthroned with sovereign power, heavenly Father exalt.

***Personal Reflection (Workplace):***

- Write your personal prayer for your workplace.

## *World*

The following verses, revealed to us by our Father in heaven, give us wisdom and understanding of the world and also for the things of the world and the things of God.

> Then the Lord said: "I am making a covenant with you. Before all your people I will do wonders never before done in any nation in all the world. The people you live among will see how awesome is the work that I, the Lord, will do for you." (Exodus 34:10)

> Let all the earth fear the Lord; let all the people of the world revere him. (Psalm 33:8)

> He said to them, "Go into all the world and preach the good news to all creation." (Mark 16:15)

> Do not love the world or anything in the world. If anyone loves the world, the love of the Father is not in him. (1 John 2:15)

> The Lord reigns forever; he has established his throne for judgment. He will judge the world in righteousness; he will govern the peoples with justice. The Lord is a refuge for the oppressed, a stronghold in times of trouble. (Psalm 9:7-9)

> For God did not send his Son into the world to condemn the world, but to save the world through him. (John 3:17)

We are meant to be citizens of heaven and pilgrims on the earth. When we are unsure of our citizenship, we are sometimes torn between our choices: Do we choose the things of the world (temporal) or the things of God (eternal)? According to Ken Boa, we are in the world, but we must walk in the world without being molded by it. Therefore, it is necessary to continually read and understand God's Word. We seek Him and pray for God's intervention in our daily walk with Him so that we will make good judgments. In 1 Timothy 6:7, we read, "For we brought nothing into the world, and we can take nothing out of it." Everything that is in the world, the longing of the flesh and of the eyes for the material things, is of the world. It is alarming that the world is becoming a powerful force to program people's minds into being attracted to everything worldly, drawing their hearts into the ungodly desires of power, wealth, and fame and drawing them farther away from the things of God.

Living in America is a great privilege and opportunity. The year was 1981 when I stepped into the land of opportunity called America. I came from a third-world country, the Philippines, where the lifestyle I experienced was just the opposite of the luxurious lifestyle we have here in America. To me, living in these two different countries instilled great moral values in my life that I learned to appreciate. I learned how to appreciate life both with and without money. The two countries complemented each other in making me the person I became. Romans 12:2 says, "Do not conform any longer to the pattern of this world, but be transformed by the renewing of your mind. Then you will be able to test and approve what God's will is—his good, pleasing and perfect will." Looking back to my childhood upbringing and exposure, I realize that God was preparing me for His vision and His purpose. In America, God enabled me to develop my life to the fullest, availing myself of the many opportunities that were part of God's underlying plan.

Although I was not born into a devout Christian family, it became a way of life for me to do what is godly and true in my relationships with others. My grandfather was the greatest influence in my life. He was a God-fearing, honest, and truthful man. In the Philippines, you are either poor or rich. I would consider my family as poor but well provided for because my mother owned a business. My childhood was simple yet significant for the way that I grew up maintaining my best behavior. I finished college in the Philippines with a degree in business. It was also in the Philippines where I got married.

My husband, a naturalized U.S. citizen, sponsored me to immigrate to America. It was an overwhelming experience and a drastic cultural change for me. Language was not much of a barrier for me, but the climate was. But I must have prepared myself well enough before I came to this country, because I was ready to tackle life head-on. My new family life seemed pretty normal and under control. Just a few lifestyle adjustments, and everything was fine. It continued to stay that way even when I started having children. Suddenly, ten years into the marriage something happened; my husband admitted to having an affair with another woman. I felt like my marriage was hit by a violent wind on a stormy day, and the relationship began to meander.

It took me years to realize that this traumatic experience would become the biggest turning point of my life. It was my wake-up call to come to Jesus and to make Him my Savior and my Lord. Psalm 107:19-21 says, "Then they cried to the Lord in their trouble, and he saved them from their distress. He sent forth his word and healed them; he rescued them from the grave. Let them give thanks to the Lord for his unfailing love and his wonderful deeds for men." I leaned on God's Word to heal and strengthen me in order to overcome this turmoil. It was then becoming real to me that God allowed this experience to happen to affirm His relationship with me. Slowly, but surely, my Father in heaven molded me into the person He wanted me to be. Indeed, with His plan for my life, I gradually became more aware of His presence, His calling, and His purpose.

Collectively, my traumatic experience, coupled with my strong-willed personality and spiced by my innovative and creative approach to my educational advancement, opened a new venture in my life. That new venture, highlighted by God's intervention, brought me into a higher arena of influence as I helped people in their financial issues and also had the opportunity to witness to them. My practice became my Father in heaven's purpose for my life. My compassion for others became a passion to a yet higher calling, and that is my passion for Jesus Christ. Writing this book was not as an intended personal goal but was instead, without any doubt, all God's calling and plan. Each day that I spent writing this book, I felt God's presence through the Holy Spirit, helping me know what to write. To be able to reach out to people all around the world, spreading God's Word, seemed to be His great purpose for this book. Undeserving, underprivileged people can be the financial benefactors of this book as well. All over the world, this book will deliver a God-driven message to all mankind on how to build a personal relationship with our Father in heaven and to grow to maturity in that relationship.

This world is a place to prepare us for the life for which God has destined us. In 1 Peter 1:16, it is written: "Be holy, because I am holy." If we are rightly related to God, our pursuit is holiness; that is our destined end. Do we believe God can come to us and make us holy? By continually restating to ourselves what the purpose of our life is and how we manifest that which God has given us, our Father in heaven will lead us to the gateway of pursuing God's mission and vision. As we live in this world, we must give account for our lives as we journey heavenward. As Paul stated in Philippians 3:14, "I press on toward the goal to win the prize for which God has called me heavenward in Christ Jesus."

***Heavenly Father:***

*Thank You for revealing Your great purpose in me.*
*Through You, Father, my life challenges shaped me*
*To be the kind of person You wanted me to be.*

*Learning my moral values from two different countries*
*Really complemented and enhanced my true sources*
*On how to value life, with or without financial resources.*

*Thank You, Father, that now You are paving the way*
*Into a wonderful, purposeful, and helpful kind of way,*
*Reaching out and spreading God's message to people globally. AMEN.*

***Heavenly Father:***

*Thank You, for the country I was born in, the Philippines, truly the pearl of the orient seas. The country's rich culture instilled in me the appreciation of nature and close family ties. The modest lifestyle helped me develop my creativity and resourcefulness. Immigrating to the United States of America enhanced my ability to explore more opportunities.*

***U**- United States of America, Land of Opportunity*
***S**- Services rendered honorably and courageously*
***A-** America, I'm proud that you are my adopted country*

*God Bless **America** and God Bless the **Philippines**. AMEN.*

***Personal Reflections (World):***

- Do you believe that God already has set a plan for you? Do you know what that plan is, and are you working on it?
- Share with fellow Christians your wisdom and understanding related to the things of the world and the things of God.
- Write your personal prayers on the subject of the world's perspectives and God's perspectives, asking God to give you wisdom to value God's eternal purpose.

***

## *Chapter Nine*

# POWER OF PRAYERS

### *The Lord's Prayer*

Matthew 18:19-20 says, "Again I tell you that if two of you on earth agree about anything you ask for, it will be done for you by my Father in heaven. For where two or three come together in my name, there am I with them." Luke 11:9-10 also says, "So I say to you: Ask and it will be given to you, seek and you will find, knock and the door will be opened to you. For everyone who asks receives, he who seeks finds, and to him who knocks, the door will be opened." Indeed, Philippians 4:6 says, "Do not be anxious about anything, but in everything, by prayer and petition, with thanksgiving, present your requests to God." It is clear that prayer is very important in our relationship with God. It is our way of communicating with Him. Through our prayers we come to know better our Father in heaven. We can just be ourselves before Him, present our requests to God and allow Him to come to us through faith and prayers. Though He does not always change things for us, God does change us in the way we look at things.

In the Matthew 6:9-13, Jesus Christ Himself gave all of us a pattern for prayer called The Lord's Prayer. This prayer is a model for how to pray. When we pray according to this pattern, we build our confidence to face any challenges that might come our way.

*Our Father in heaven,*
*hallowed be Your name,*
*Your kingdom come,*

*Your will be done*
*on earth as it is in heaven.*
*Give us today our daily bread.*
*Forgive us our debts,*
*as we also have forgiven our debtors.*
*And lead us not into temptation,*
*but deliver us from the evil one.*

Though lots of us have recited this prayer many times, do we grasp its real meaning? To be able to deliver truthfully every word of the prayer, we must understand all the components and their meanings.

***1. "Our Father in Heaven."*** God created us, and He owns everything. Genesis 1:1 says, "In the beginning God created the heavens and the earth." Therefore, He is above everything in heaven and earth. He wants us to approach Him as "Daddy." We are His family, and He desires intimacy with His children. His love and grace is supreme. When we pray, we must first praise and honor God. Psalm 100:4 says, "Enter his gates with thanksgiving and his courts with praise; give thanks to him and praise his name."

***2. "Hallowed be your name."*** God is holy, majestic, and magnificent. First Peter 1:16 says, "For it is written: 'Be holy, because I am holy.'" We must give reverence to God. He wants us to be transformed into His likeness with ever-increasing glory. When we pray, we must acknowledge His *holiness*. We hallow God by acknowledging Him as *Jehovah Tsidkenu* (The Lord our righteousness); *Jehovah M'Kaddesh* (The Lord who sanctifies); *Jehovah Shalom* (The Lord who is our peace); *Jehovah Shammah* (The Lord is there; He never leaves us); *Jehovah Rophe* (The Lord who heals); *Jehovah Jireh* (The Lord will provide); *Jehovah Nissi* (The Lord is my banner); and *Jehovah Rohi* (The Lord who is my shepherd).

***3. "Your Kingdom Come, your will be done on earth as it is in heaven."*** God loves us so much that He wants us to experience His glory on earth. Genesis 1:27 says, "So God created man in his own image, in the image of God he created him; male and female he created them." He wants us to be Christlike so that He can use us for His glory. Therefore, we must submit to Him. We must allow God to be in control of our lives and to lead us to life everlasting. When we pray, we ask Him to reveal His priorities and His purpose in us and we ask that His will be done in us, through us, and upon us. But let us always remember, it is His will that is to be done, not our will. Matthew 6:33 says, "But seek first his kingdom and his righteousness, and all these things will be given to you as well."

***4. "Give us today our daily bread."*** God provides for our needs. John 16:24 says, "Until now you have not asked for anything in my name. Ask and you will receive, and your joy will be complete." When we pray, we ask for His *provision* and sustenance for our daily needs. We must learn to ask God for what we need for each day, confident that He knows our daily need. Sometimes we ask for God's provision for the wrong motives; so let us not get frustrated if we don't receive what we ask for. Remember also that our requests and petitions must be in accordance with His will.

***5. "Forgive us our debts as we also have forgiven our debtors."*** God's love for us was supremely demonstrated by sending Jesus Christ to die for our sins. Jesus showed us the true meaning of humility by dying on the cross for the forgiveness of our sins. Matthew 6:14-15 says, "For if you forgive men when they sin against you, your heavenly Father will also forgive you. But if you do not forgive men their sins, your Father will not forgive your sins." When we ask for God's *forgiveness,* we also must make sure that we forgive those who have wronged us. An unforgiving heart will put us into a heavy bondage of life problems. The power of forgiveness is an essential tool to release us from that bondage. Nehemiah 9:17

says, "But you are a forgiving God, gracious and compassionate, slow to anger and abounding in love."

***6. "And lead us not into temptation."*** God created us, and He is in control of our lives, but it is our responsibility to be on guard for temptation. When we pray, we must ask for God's *protection* so that we won't succumb to temptation. We must be careful because we are being tempted every day. Hebrews 2:18 says, "Because he himself suffered when he was tempted, he is able to help those who are being tempted." God should be the stronghold in our challenges and the safeguard against temptation.

***7. "But deliver us from the evil one."*** God already redeemed us from our sins and from the bondage of the Evil One, Satan. When we pray, we rebuke the Evil One, as we proclaim God as our Lord and Savior. Psalm 56:9 says, "Then my enemies will turn back when I call for help. By this I will know that God is for me."

# From A to Z
# Collection of Prayers

**A**

**Heavenly Father:**

Above the heaven and earth You're supremely divine.
All to your creations here on earth You surely shine,
Adhering to Your power and love exceedingly fine,
Administering Your plan relating to mine seemingly intertwine.
AMEN.

***References:***

*Chapter 1 (Who Am I to God?-Vision for Life)*
*Chapter 2 (Building Relationship-Personal Relationship with God)*

**B**

**Heavenly Father:**

Before I surrendered my life to You, Almighty,
Bearing so many problems I felt so unhappy,
Behold I come to worship and honor your glory,
Blessings poured immensely for me and my family.
AMEN.

***References:***

*Chapter 1 (Who Am I to God?-Gift of Salvation)*
*Chapter 3 (God-Driven Purpose-Worship)*

**C**

**Heavenly Father:**

Creating mankind to pursue heavenly purpose,
Channeling their heart to a much-desired focus,
Character development to man assuredly impose,
Captivating God's truth wakens man's repose.
AMEN.

***References:***
*Chapter 1 (Who Am I to God?-Vision for Life)*
*Chapter 6 (Commitment to Character Development)*

## D

Dear **Heavenly Father**, please hear my intense crying,
Daunting miseries that seemed overwhelming,
Dealing with marital problems that inflicted me with suffering,
Develop in me the spirit of wisdom to ease my agonizing.
AMEN.

***References:***
*Chapter 1 (Who Am I to God?-Personal Encounter with the Lord)*
*Chapter 2 (Building Relationship-Family Relationship: Spouse)*

## E

**Heavenly Father:**
Entrusted by Your grace is Your way of redeeming.
Enhanced by Your mercy provided us spiritual blessing.
Everlasting life You promised gave us true meaning.
Endless love You gave, I now proclaim life's worth living!
AMEN.

***References:***
*Chapter 1 (Who Am I to God?-The Gift of Salvation)*
*Chapter 2 (Building Relationship-Personal Relationship with God)*

## F

**Heavenly Father, You are:**
Faithful and true forever I worship You.
Far and away I will always be near You.
From east to west I only set my eyes on You.
From north to south I will continue to seek You.
AMEN.

***References:***
*Chapter 1 (Building Relationship-Personal Relationship with God)*
*Chapter 3 (God-Driven Purpose-Worship)*

## G

**Heavenly Father:**
Gone were those old days that I longed for Thee,
Giving me hope and future that I couldn't see.
Grace came to redeem me, and now I'm set free,
God's wisdom and blessing overflowing in me.
AMEN.
***Reference:***
*Chapter 1 (Who Am I to God?-The Gift of Salvation)*

## H

**Heavenly Father, Your:**
Holiness in You we must greatly proclaim.
Hail, holy King, we must boldly claim.
Hallowed be Thy name, we gladly exclaim.
Heaven is your throne we proudly acclaim.
AMEN.
***Reference:***
*Chapter 3 (God-Driven Purpose-Worship)*

## I

**Heavenly Father:**
In my heart God became part of me.
In my eyes God showed me the way.
In my lips God proclaimed His word.
In my mind God instilled the truth.
AMEN.
***Reference:***
*Chapter 2 (Building Relationship-Personal Relationship with God)*

**<u>J</u>**

**Heavenly Father:**

Joyfully and true Your Word should be read,
Jollity to all nations where it could be heard.
Joy to the world, a song always remembered,
Jesus born in Bethlehem must be endeared
AMEN

***Reference:***

*Chapter 3 (God-Driven Purpose-Worship)*

**<u>K</u>**

**Heavenly Father:**

Kindness and faithfulness adorn You, Lord Almighty,
Kingdom impact known to men seeking Your glory.
Knowledge and wisdom You provided abundantly,
Knowing and loving You we did so passionately.
AMEN.

***References:***

*Chapter 2 (Building Relationship-Personal Relationship with God)*
*Chapter 3 (Who Am I to God?-Living with Passion)*

**<u>L</u>**

**Heavenly Father:**

Love, faith, and hope are godly virtues;
Loving Father You entrusted to us those clues.
Lovingly and passionately I must pursue,
Looking into what you ask me to rescue.
AMEN.

***References:***

*Chapter 5 (Call to Godly Virtues-Love, Faith, and Hope)*
*Chapter 1 (Who Am I to God?-Vision for Life)*

**M**

**Heavenly Father:**
My love for Your mighty strength is my stronghold.
My everyday challenges, they are about to unfold.
My peace and joy seemed threatened if not truthfully told.
My Lord, forgive me if my worries I withhold.
AMEN.
*Reference:*
*Chapter 6 (Commitment to Character Development-Forgiveness)*

**N**

**Heavenly Father:**
Nothing will ever be done without Your presence,
O grateful God.
Nonetheless, apart from You I will absolutely get lost,
O truthful God.
Now that You're here to stay in my heart and soul,
O faithful God,
Never again will I let You out of my sight,
O merciful God.
AMEN.
***Reference:***
*Chapter 2 (Building Relationship-Personal Relationship with God)*

**O**

**Heavenly Father:**
Over the mountains and over the hills,
Off You go to create some more thrills.
Only for men to prove and show your skill,
O Lord, You are glorified because this is Your will.
AMEN.
***Reference:***
*Chapter 3 (God-Driven Purpose-Worship)*

**P**

**Heavenly Father:**

Perfect harmony You blended each family.
Parent and children are united every day.
Patience and perseverance are in their way,
Partaking of Your words that guide them all day.
AMEN.

***Reference:***

*Chapter 2 (Building Relationship-Family Relationship)*

**Q**

**Heavenly Father:**

Questions unanswered come along as time passes by.
Quarrels sometimes disturb us, although they heal as time goes by.
Quitting God's great purpose hopefully won't happen or come by.
Quality time together with God asking for forgiveness is worth a try.
AMEN.

***References:***

*Chapter 6 (Commitment to Character Development-Forgiveness)*
*Chapter 2 (Building Relationship-Personal Relationship with God)*

**R**

**Heavenly Father:**

Responsibility, humility, integrity, and honesty are godly acts,
Referring to our daily activities and in the way we simply act.
Remembering God's commands that we shall remain intact,
Rendering true services to others and being accountable is a fact.
AMEN.

***Reference:***

*Chapter 6 (Commitment to Character Development)*

**S**

**Heavenly Father:**

Sometimes unwillingly one submits to a trap of ungodly desires;
Somehow undoubtedly one clearly knows that consequences arise.
So then ask for God's uncompromising forgiveness as it transpires;
Sadness and sorrow slowly depart from a man's heart as he testifies.
AMEN.

***References:***

*Chapter 1 (Who am I to God?-Personal Encounter with the Lord)*
*Chapter 2 (Building Relationship-Family Relationship)*

**T**

**Heavenly Father:**

Today is the beginning of a brand-new day,
Truly to serve God and others as He would portray.
Tomorrow is yet to come for another pathway;
Therefore we ask God's guidance as we begin to pray.
AMEN.

***Reference:***

*Chapter 1 (Who Am I to God?-Every Day Is a New Beginning)*

**U**

**Heavenly Father:**

Understanding between the world's kingdom and God's kingdom
Unfolds as your choices come, when priorities are set with freedom.
Unsure but true, the world's kingdom gives value to the world's economy;

Undoubtedly God's kingdom gives value to those with God's priority.
AMEN.
***Reference:***
*Chapter 4 (Lifestyle: Is God in Control?-Financial/Wealth)*

**V**
**Heavenly Father:**
Verily, verily, as I say unto God,
Victory hails as I proclaim unto God
Vision and mission as they come and go,
Virtues and character develop as we go.
AMEN.
***References:***
*Chapter 5 (Call to Godly Virtues)*
*Chapter 6 (Commitment to Character Development)*

**W**
**Heavenly Father:**
With Your guidance and protection I shall not fear;
With Your teaching of Thy Word I surely bear.
With my prayer I fervently offer without smear,
With my faith in You, my God, I solemnly adhere.
AMEN.
***References***
*Chapter 2 (Building Relationship-Personal Relationship with God)*
*Chapter 5 (Call to Godly Virtues)*

**Y**
**Heavenly Father:**
Yesterday is gone, never to come back,
Yet there's still tomorrow to bring a new fact.
Young and old it seems are easy to distract;
Your love and mercy will get them on track.
AMEN.

***Reference:***
*Chapter 1 (Who Am I to God-Every Day Is a New Beginning)*

**Z**
**Heavenly Father:**
Zeal for living each day as we should have with Jesus
Zealously demonstrated in our daily walk with Jesus,
Zest with pizzazz enhances our relationship with Jesus,
Zestfully embedded in our solemn purpose with Jesus.
AMEN.
*Reference:*
*Chapter 2 (Building Relationship-Personal Relationship with God)*

## *In Jesus Christ's Name, Amen!*

**I** - I worship and adore
**N** - Name that symbolizes holiness

**J** - Jesus Christ the heavenly King proclaim
**E** - Everlasting gift of salvation now acclaim
**S** - Suffering and dying on the cross
**U** - Unfolds mighty kingdom's purpose
**S** - Surrender to God by all mankind at His cost

**C** - Commitment to kingdom authority
**H** - Honesty to oneself and to everybody
**R** - Respect and honor to humanity
**I** - Integrity is in our words and actions
**S** - Self-control overrules our emotion
**T** - Trustworthy as well with our possessions
**S** - Service to mankind worthy of all praise

**N** - Name worthy beyond compare
**A** - Almighty and all-knowing
**M** - Majestic and magnificent
**E** - Everlasting and eternal

**A** - Almighty Father in heaven
**M** - Magnified by all Your creation
**E** - Excellent is Your name
**N** - Now and forever

# AUTHOR'S BIOGRAPHY
# Teresita "*Tess*" Paje, MBA

**Business Philosophy:** To build a lifelong business relationship with clients based on Bible-driven financial strategies.

Tess Paje is a financial advisor and a member of a professional group called Kingdom Advisors, who seeks to integrate Biblical principles in their profession. She earned her undergraduate degree in accounting in the Philippines and her Masters in Business Administration degree with an emphasis in financial management at San Diego. Married for nearly thirty years to Rey, a registered nurse, they are blessed with two children, Trisha, a graduate of the University of San Diego, and Karina, a graduate of the University of California at Los Angeles.

Her work experience as an accountant and auditor gave her an interest in helping people in their financial problems, which later became her passion as a financial advisor. Driven by this passion for helping people, she was inspired to organize the San Diego Premier Lions Club, a humanitarian organization. What she envisions for the club is seen in the acronym PREMIER—a Person who Respects an Excellent Mentor with Innovative Empowered Responsibilities.

Tess Paje's passion is helping people in their financial and life planning. Her love for the Lord gave her the vision to start the Maranatha Businesswomen's Bible Study Group. This is a support group for women who want to grow in maturity in their relationship with the Lord. Tess believes that to grow strong in our relationship with our Lord, we must spend time in His

Word, in prayer, in discipleship, and in fellowship. Her vision statement for the Maranatha Businesswomen's Bible Study Group is: To engage, equip, and empower women to apply Biblical principles in their God-given callings, thereby enabling them to manage their time, talents, abilities, and material resources in accordance with God's plan in their lives and in the lives of others, thus ultimately glorifying God. Tess Paje conducts seminars and presentations and is a public speaker. Her most memorable and rewarding speaking engagement was at "Practically Speaking Conference," a Maranatha Women in Ministry Conference, with her topic on financial stewardship.

Her compassion for people has become her passion to serve Jesus Christ. God's promise in Jeremiah 29:11-13 highlighted this passion:

> *"For I know the plans I have for you," declares the Lord, "plans to prosper you and not to harm you, plans to give you hope and a future. Then you will call upon me and come and pray to me, and I will listen to you. You will seek me and find me when you seek me with all your heart."*

www.ingramcontent.com/pod-product-compliance
Lightning Source LLC
LaVergne TN
LVHW090956080826
845145LV00003B/1022

* 9 7 8 1 9 3 6 0 7 6 1 2 3 *